American Manners and Customs

(A Guide for Newcomers)

The Best of
Easy English
NEWS

#1

by

Elizabeth Claire

Illustrated by Dave Nicholson

Eardley Publications

Developmental Editors: Sally Isaacs and Steve Jorgensen
Copy Editor: George A. Rowland

Design: Steve Jorgensen
Illustrations and Cover Design: Dave Nicholson

©2004 Eardley Publications
302 Nedellec Drive
Saddle Brook, NJ 07663 USA

Printed in the United States of America.

ISBN: 0937630-11-X

This book is dedicated to *you*,
the Newcomer.

Welcome!

**Other Books
by Elizabeth Claire**

Hi! (English for Children)
ESL Wonder Workbook # 1: This Is Me
ESL Wonder Workbook # 2: All Around Me
The New Boy Is Lost! (Where Is Taro?)

What's So Funny?
Dangerous English 2000!

Three Little Words: A, An, and The
ESL Teacher's Activities Kit
ESL Teacher's Holiday Activities Kit
Help Your Buddy Learn English

Just A Minute! (language game)

Easy English NEWS, a monthly newspaper for newcomers to the United States:

With co-author Judie Haynes:
Classroom Teacher's ESL Survival Kit #1
Classroom Teacher's ESL Survival Kit #2

Photo: David Derex Studios

Dear Reader,

My grandmother, Elizabeth Skrinar, came to the United States from Slovakia, at the age of 14, to work as a maid. That was in 1904, more than a hundred years ago.

As a child, I loved to hear her tell the stories of her first years in the United States. She had a terrible trip to America. She had trouble with the English language. She was embarrassed when she did or said the wrong things. She didn't understand American manners and customs.

My grandmother lived to a wonderful old age of 96. Yet she never forgot the troubles of those early years. She always laughed as she told her stories. "But at *that* time," she said, "these things were not funny at all."

Years later, I became an ESL teacher. I spent many years listening to my students' problems. I answered their questions about American manners, customs, holidays, culture, day-to-day life, and citizenship. Finally, I decided to write a monthly newspaper, *Easy English NEWS*. The purpose was to help newcomers feel more welcome here in the United States.

Easy English NEWS had a monthly column called "Culture Corner." Readers told me it was their favorite column. It helped them to see "the invisible things" that Americans expect from each other. It helped them to know what to do and what to say in many situations.

This book, *American Manners and Customs* is a collection of the best of *Easy English NEWS* Culture Corner Articles. I had fun putting the book together for you. I hope it helps you. I'd love to hear your comments and stories about your own problems with American manners. Write to:

Eardley Publications
P.O. Box 2596
Fair Lawn, New Jersey 07410

—or send an email to: ESL@elizabethclaire.com

For other books to help English language learners, visit my website:
www.Elizabethclaire.com

Sincerely,
Elizabeth Claire

CONTENTS

Elizabeth Claire
earned her B.A.
in Spanish and Education from
the City College of New York,
and her M.A.
in Teaching English as a Second Language
from New York University.
She has taught
English to newcomers for 35 years.

What do I say? What do I do?

Welcome to the United States!

You notice that people's behavior is different from yours. You wonder about it. Are these Americans being **rude***? You worry about it too—Are *you* being rude? You feel a language **barrier*** *and* a culture barrier. You want to feel a part of your new country. You wonder if that will ever happen.

Manners are different in different countries. This book was written to explain the **invisible*** things Americans expect from each other. It will open the doors so you can feel fully a part of your new country.

The U.S. is a large country, with people from all over the world. In this short book, we'll explain the most common manners and customs you might find among many Americans. But remember, there are differences in each part of the country. There are differences between younger people and older people. There are differences between educated and less educated, between city and country, and between rich and poor.

It's your job to observe the people around you. Ask your teachers, and your American friends and neighbors, to explain manners in the **situations*** you find yourself in.

What are manners?

Manners are the ways that help us get along in a group. Good manners means thinking about the needs of others and the feelings of others. Our manners let other people know that we are trying to be friendly and helpful. Good manners make life easy.

Where do American manners come from? Some of our customs are many hundreds of years old. In 1922, Emily Post wrote a 687-page book called *Etiquette* * *for Society and Business*. It was very popular then. It became the guide for American middle-class and upper-class manners. People still read it and follow the rules she wrote about.

However, manners have changed over the years. The publishers of Emily Post have had to change her book many times to keep up-to-date.

Americans are generally very **informal***. It's part of the American belief that everyone is equal. We hope you will feel more comfortable and **at ease*** after reading this little book.

Word Help

rude *adjective*. Bad-mannered. Not polite.
barrier *noun*. A wall or fence to keep a person out.
invisible *adjective*. Cannot be seen.
situation *noun*. Condition that a person is in: place, problem, activity, and other people.

etiquette *noun*. A set of rules, customs, principles and manners for social behavior.
at ease *prepositional phrase*. Relaxed; not worried.
informal *adjective*. Casual, not official; ordinary, without strict rules that everyone must follow in exactly the same way.

1. Please. Thank You. You're Welcome. Excuse Me. I'm sorry.

These are among the first words a child learns in English. They will be the most useful words for you in English, too.

You have to learn when to say them, and how much to say them.

The word *please* can go at the beginning or at the end of a sentence. *Please pass the salt.* Or, *Pass the salt, please.*

To be more **polite***, *"may I"* or *"could you"* are often used: *"Could you pass the salt, please?"*

"Give me a pencil, please," sounds too direct, like a **command***. *"May I please have a pencil?"* seems softer, and less direct.

"Could you please close the window?" sounds more polite than *"Close the window, please."* The words alone do not make the sentence polite. A lot of the feeling of politeness is in your **tone of voice*** when you ask for something.

Americans like to be **appreciated***. The size of the "thank you" depends on the size of the gift or favor:

Thanks. (Someone **lent*** you a pencil, or held a door for you.)

Thanks a lot. (Someone *gave* you a pencil, or held a very heavy door for you.)

Thank you. (Someone paid you a **compliment***, or gave you a seat on a bus.)

*Thank you very, **very** much*. (Someone did you a favor that was very helpful. Someone found your keys and returned them.)

*Thank you **so** much*. (Someone did a favor that surprised you and made your life easier.)

I really appreciate this so much. How can I ever thank you enough? You are a saint. (Someone has stopped on the road and repaired your **flat tire***.)

This is so wonderful. I couldn't have done this without you. Thank you so much. I'll never forget it.

Don't **overdo*** it. For a *small* favor, *one* "please" and *one* "thank you" are enough.

When someone says *"Thank you"* the normal **response*** is *"You're welcome."*

Word Help

polite *adjective*. Having good manners; kind, courteous.
command *noun*. An order from a general or captain to a person of lesser power.
tone of voice *noun phrase*. The quality of a person's voice. A tone can be soft, gentle, friendly, and pleasant, or angry, sarcastic, harsh, and threatening,
appreciate *verb*. To show or tell a person that you are thankful for their gift or favor.

lend *verb*. (past form: lent) To let another person use something that belongs to you.
compliment 1. *noun*. A word or words that say something nice about a person. 2. *verb*. To tell a person that you think he or she is good, kind, beautiful, etc.
flat tire *noun*. A car's tire that has a hole and has lost its air.
overdo *verb*. To do more than needed.
response *noun*. Answer.

2

We can also say *"It was [or is] my pleasure."* *"Think nothing of it."* Or *"No problem."*

If we were very happy to do a favor for someone, we might say, *"You're perfectly welcome."* Or *"There's no need to thank me; the **pleasure*** was mine."*

Americans say *excuse me* or *pardon me* in many **situations***:

- to **apologize*** for making an unpleasant noise, burp, **belch***, hiccup, cough, or passing gas (flatulence)

- to apologize for **disturbing*** someone

- to apologize for bumping into a person accidentally

- to apologize for walking between two people who are speaking.

- to **interrupt*** a conversation

- to get someone's attention so we can ask a question

- to ask a person to repeat something we didn't understand

- to correct ourselves when we said something that was a mistake.

- to leave a conversation to go do something else.

Word Help

pleasure *noun*. Good, happy feeling.
situation *noun*. Condition; what is happening at the moment.
apologize *verb*. To say that you are sorry for something you did or said.
belch *noun*. A loud noise of gas coming up from the stomach through the mouth.
disturb *verb*. To make noises or do things that will annoy people.
interrupt *verb*. To stop someone's conversation in order to speak.

A person might say *"Excuse ME!"* **sarcastically*** when another person says something that the first person didn't like.

"I beg your pardon" may mean *"I didn't hear you."*

"I'm sorry" is used when you feel bad that another person was hurt in some way. You apologize for accidents that you caused, or accidental rudeness.

"I'm sorry." (You ate the last cookie, and your friend wanted one.)

"I'm sorry. I was wrong." (You want to make up after a disagreement you had with your neighbor.)

"I'm terribly sorry. Are you OK?" (You ran over someone's foot with your shopping cart at the supermarket.)

"I'm truly sorry. I didn't want to hurt you." (You are breaking up with your girlfriend, and she feels terrible about it.)

*"I'm **dreadfully*** sorry."* (You have spilled ink on someone's jacket.)

Sometimes *"I'm sorry,"* is not enough. Offer to fix the problem you caused. *"Please let me pay for your cleaning bill."*

Respond to the person who says *"I'm sorry"*:

"That's OK. No harm done."

"That did hurt. But don't worry about it. I'll be OK in a minute."

"Thanks for offering to pay the bill. I'll let you know how much it is."

sarcastically *adverb*. Said in a way that is the opposite of what you mean. This shows you are annoyed, or is an unkind joke.
dreadfully *adverb*. An intensifier: very, *very*.

3

Let's talk about it.

1. What are the most common polite words in English? What are the most common polite words in your native language?

2. How would you make these requests more polite?

   a. Give me a cup of coffee.

   b. Close the door.

   c. Lend me a pen.

   d. Help me do this.

3. Tell how you would thank a person who has:

   a. Helped open a door for you.

   b. Found your eyeglasses and returned them to you.

   c. Given you a new winter coat.

   d. Helped fix a computer problem that took an hour to solve.

4. An elderly lady has thanked you for helping to find her lost dog. What will you respond?

5. Pretend you received an expensive silver picture frame for a wedding gift. What will you write on a thank-you card?

6. What are some reasons for you to say "Excuse me"? When would you say "I'm sorry"?

4

Using new words:
Match the word with its meaning.

_____ 7. to break into other people's conversation

_____ 8. to do more than is needed

_____ 9. to say the name of a person or object during a conversation or speech

_____ 10. to show or tell a person that you are thankful for their gift or favor

_____ 11. to tell a person that you think he or she has done a good job, or looks good, or is wearing nice clothing, etc.

_____ 12. a good and happy feeling

_____ 13. to say that you are sorry for something that hurt another person in some way

_____ 14. speaking in a way in which the speaker says the opposite of what he means in order to show that he is annoyed

A. compliment

B. pleasure

C. interrupt

D. overdo

E. sarcastically

F. apologize

G. mention

H. appreciate

Write a word in each sentence to make it correct. Choose from this list: compliment, appreciated, end, overdo.

15. You can use the word "please" at the beginning or at the _____ of a sentence.

16. Americans like to be _____ for favors or gifts.

17. If someone pays you a _____, you can say "thank you."

18. It's not necessary to _____ the thank you's. One "thank you" is enough for a small favor.

5

What's your name?

This seems like a simple question. But it isn't. Many newcomers are confused about American names.

The first thing that can confuse people is the order of American names. Our **given name*'** (the personal name) comes first. Examples: George, Anna, Sally, Robert. We call it our *first name.*

The **family name***, or **surname***, comes last. Americans call the family name the *last name.* Example: Washington, Smith, O'Brien, Johnson, Garcia.

However: When we want a list of names to put in alphabetical order, we ask people to "Write your name, last name first:" Washington, George. Then we use a comma to separate the two names.

Many people have one or more **middle name.*** We often also use a **nickname*** instead of our given names.

The second thing that confuses people is when to use the last name, and when to use the given name. In **informal*** situations, Americans use first names. Neighbors, students, and other "equals" are introduced by their first names. A person you just met may say, *"Please call me [Elizabeth]."* You may invite them to call you by your first name, too.

Many Americans think young people should show **respect*** to older people, employers, and teachers. That means: use their **title*** and last name.

In **formal*** situations we use titles with people's last names. For example:

Mr. /*mister*/ Brown

Mrs. /*missiz*/ Hill

Miss Jones

Ms /*miz*/ Green

The title *Miss* is **traditionally*** for unmarried women. The title *Mrs.* is used for married women. *Mr.* is used for men.

The word *Mr.* does not show if a man is married or not. About 1970, women began to ask "Why should our title tell if we are married or not?" So, today many women prefer the title *Ms.*

Ms can be used by both married and unmarried women. You can use this title safely when you don't know if a woman is married or not.

Traditionally, when a woman married, she stopped using her **maiden name.*** She took her husband's name. *Miss Mary Jones* became *Mrs. John Brown.*

Today's young women ask, "Men don't have to change their name when they get married; why should

Word Help

given name *noun.* A name that parents choose for a child—such as John, Miguel, Anna, Jessica.
family name *noun.* The father's last name. His a wife and children usually use it as their last name.
surname [suhr/ naym] Same as the family name.
middle name *noun.* A name between the first name and last name. It is a second given name. It may also be a family name, such as the mother's maiden name.
nickname *noun.* An unofficial name that has been given to a person.
informal *adjective.* Casual, not official; ordinary, day-to-day.

respect *noun.* A showing of honor and good manners towards another person.
title *noun.* A word such as *Mr., Mrs., Ms., Miss, Dr., Professor,* etc. used before a person's name.
formal *adjective.* Following fixed rules of dress or behavior.
traditionally *adverb.* According to the way things have been done for many years in the past.
maiden name *noun.* A woman's last name before she is married.

I have to change *my* name?" Now, many women keep their maiden names after they get married. Ms. Mary Jones remains Ms. Mary Jones even after she marries John Brown.

A woman may use her own family name as well as her husband's family name. *Ms. Mary Jones* may become *Ms. Mary Jones-Brown.* Their children may have both family names, or just the father's family name.

Is this confusing?

It certainly is. Americans get confused, too. They are not sure how to address a newly married woman, so they have to ask, "Are you keeping your maiden name?" Or "What name will you be using?"

When you write a person's address on a letter, write the person's title, the given name, and the family name: *Mr. John Brown; Ms. Mary Brown.* When you address the envelope to both the husband and the wife, you can write *Mr. and Mrs. John Brown.* Or they may ask you to write *John Brown and Mary Jones.*

The title *Doctor* (Dr.) is used for people with advanced education (6-8 years of university study). This includes medical doctors, chiropractors, dentists, and some scientists, teachers, and others. (Not every *Dr.* is a *medical doctor*!

The title *Professor* (Prof.) is used for a senior teacher at a university. *Reverend* (Rev.) is a title used for a minister of a church. *Father* is the title for a Catholic priest. *Monsignor* [mahn seen′ yuhr] is the title for an officer in the Catholic Church. The title for a **nun*** is *Sister.* The supervisor of a group of nuns is *Mother Superior.* The title for the leader of a Jewish congregation is *Rabbi* [ra biy]

For people who are important in the government, we use titles such as *Judge, Senator,* and *President,* with family names. A lawyer may use the term *Esquire* (*Esq.*) after his name.

Word Help

nun [nuhn] *noun*. A "sister" in a religious order who does not marry, and lives a life serving her church and God.

Let's talk about it.

1. What is your family name? Do you have a maiden name?

2. What is your given name? Do you have a middle name?

   What is your title?

3. How do you say your name in your native language? Which name comes first? How do you write it?

4. What titles do people use in your native language? Do the titles tell if a person is married or not?

5. When a woman marries in your native country, how does her name change? What name will her children have?

6. What titles do Americans use for a man and his wife? What titles do you use in your native country?

7. When a woman marries in the United States, how does her name change? What last name will her children have?

8. A woman's name is Dr. Barbara Wheeler. Is she a medical doctor?

9. What was the most surprising thing in this lesson for you?

Using new words:

Match the word with its meaning.

_____ 10. important or serious places or events are _____

_____ 11. a woman's family name before she is married

_____ 12. a person who sees that a group of workers do their work correctly

_____ 13. a word such as Miss, Mr., Mrs., Dr.

_____ 14 family name

_____ 15. a woman who lives in a religious group to serve God

_____ 16. casual, relaxed, without strict rules

_____ 17. The first name, in the U.S., is the

_____

A. nun

B. last name

C. formal

D. title

E. supervisor

F. maiden name

G. informal

H. given name

18. The title _____ can be used for both married and unmarried women.

19. When Miss Joan Smith marries Mr. David Wilson, her name may become _____ or _____ or _____ or _____ or _____.

20. What is the best title for these people? Choose from this list: *Mrs., Reverend, Sister, Father, Dr., Professor, Rabbi.*

a. _____ Lee is a dentist.

b. _____ Hill is a senior teacher at a university.

c. _____ Maria is a nun in the Roman Catholic church.

d. _____ Rosenbloom is the leader of a Jewish temple.

e. _____ Jackson is the minister of a Baptist church.

f. _____ Bob Jones is the wife of Mr. Bob Jones.

g. _____ O'Malley is a priest in a Catholic church.

9

American Names, Part II

What shall we name the baby?

Americans may name their newborn child for a grandparent, aunt, uncle, or other relative. They may give the baby the name of a family friend, or some person who is important in the parents' lives. Some babies are named for famous people, **saints***, Bible heroes, movie stars, or sports stars. It's common for a child to have two given names.

When a boy is named for his father, his name has the word "**Junior***" after it. (The **abbreviation*** is *Jr.*) The father's name then has the word "**Senior***" after it (abbreviated "*Sr.*"). It is *not* common for a *girl* to be named after her mother.

The most common names given to baby boys in the year 2002 were Jacob, Michael, Joshua, Andrew, Ethan, Joseph, Christopher, Daniel, Nicholas, William, Anthony, David, Tyler, Alexander, Ryan, John, and James.

The most common names for girls were Emily, Madison, Hannah, Alexis, Ashley, Abigail, Sarah, Samantha, Olivia, Elizabeth, Alyssa, Kayla, Alexis, Jessica, Taylor, Anna, Lauren, and Megan.

Some of these names have been popular for hundreds of years. Other names are new.

Most names have meanings. For example, Michael is a **Hebrew*** word that means "he who is like God." Most people do not know the meanings of their names.

Some new parents pick out a name from a book of names. Other parents want an uncommon name for their child. They **invent*** a name!

Does a person's name tell whether the person is a male or a female?

Usually, but not always. There are names and **nicknames*** that are used for both sexes. For example: Jess, Jamie, Pat, Leslie, Jackie, Jordan, Lee, Taylor, and Chris. In other cases, boys' and girls' names may sound the same, but are spelled differently. Toni, Jeanne, Billie, and Bobbie are girls' names. Tony, Gene, Billy, and Bobby are boys' names.

Some girls' names are based on boys' names: Robert, Roberta; Gabriel, Gabrielle; Daniel, Danielle; Steve, Stephanie; Alexander, Alexandra; Joseph, Josephine; Patrick, Patricia.

In England, the custom of having family names began in the 1300s. These **surnames*** were often taken from the person's occupation or location, or a physical characteristic: The most

Word Help

saint *noun*. A person with a special relationshp with God, according to the Roman Catholic church.
junior *adjective*. Younger; the son.
abbreviation *noun*. A short written form.
senior *adjective*. Older; the father.

Hebrew *noun*. The people and language of the Jews.
invent *verb*. To make something up; to create a new thing.
nickname *noun*. A short form of a name, or a familiar name that a person is called. *Mike* is a nickname for Michael. *Betty and Liz are* nicknames for Elizabeth.
surname *noun*. Family name.
metal *noun*. A hard, shiny material such as silver, gold, brass, iron, tin, copper, etc.

common American family name is Smith. A *smith* is a person who works with **metal***, such as black*smith* (iron), tin*smith*, gold*smith*, and silver*smith*.

Other common English family names in the U.S. are Johnson, Williams, Jones, Brown, Davis, Wilson, Taylor, Anderson, Thomas, Jackson, White, and Thompson. A person with one of these last names might be white or black. (Many African slaves took their last name from the name of their white owners.)

The most common Hispanic names in the U.S. are Garcia, Martinez, Rodriguez, Hernandez, Lopez, Gonzales, Perez, Sanchez, Rivera, Ramirez, Diaz, Ortiz, and Gomez.

Some people change their name. Movie stars and writers often give themselves beautiful names. Business people choose names that are easy to pronounce and easy to remember.

Should you change your name?

You can, if you want to. It is legal to use any name you like. (As long as it is not for the purpose of **fraud***.) However, you should sign your important **documents***, checks, licenses, test papers, and school records with the name on your passport, your **birth certificate,*** or your marriage document. If you have your name legally changed in court, you can use your new name on your documents.

Years ago, it was common for immigrants to choose an American first name. Now it is more common for immigrants to keep their name.

Word Help

fraud *noun*. The crime of cheating or stealing by pretending to be a different person.
document *noun*. Important paper.
birth certificate *noun*. The document with information about a baby's birth time, place, and parents

Let's talk about it.

1. Tell how Americans choose names for their babies.

2. How are babies' names chosen in your home country?

3. Who named you? Why do you have the name you have?

4. Does your name have a meaning? Tell about it.

5. Do you like your name? Have you ever wanted to change it?

6. What does the word "Junior" mean after a person's name?

7. What are the most popular names for babies in the United States recently?

8. What are some popular given names in your native country?

9. What are some American names that can be for either a boy or a girl? Does this happen in your native language?

10. What are the girls names that are based on these boys' names: Robert? Daniel? Alexander? Joseph? Patrick?

11. What are some common family names in the U.S? What are some common family names in your home country?

Using new words:
Match the word with its meaning.

_____ 12. job, career

_____ 13. older, or father

_____ 14. feeling of self-worth

_____ 15. younger, or son

_____ 16. important paper

_____ 17. A name that is not an official name, but used by one's friends

_____ 18. to say a word, but with the wrong sound

A. junior

B. senior

C. occupation

D. nickname

E. mispronounce

F. pride

G. document

Write a word in each sentence to make it correct. Choose from this list:
pronounce, Smith, relative, girls, names, father, remember.

19. Some people name their babies for a grandparent, aunt, uncle, or other

    _____.

20. When a boy is named for his _____, his name has Jr. after it.

21. It's common for a child to have two given _____.

22. Some names are used for both boys and _____.

23. The most common American family name is

    _____.

24. Business people might choose a name that is easier to

    _____ and _____.

25. The most interesting thing I learned in this lesson:

    _____

Meeting People

The **first impression*** you give others is important to your later relationship. "Body language" is a very important part of a first impression. We remember the way you dress, move, shake hands, and look at us. These things can be more important than what you *say*.

Stand up when you are **introduced*** to another person. Standing shows that you are interested in meeting the other person. Look directly at the person you are meeting.

Shake hands with a strong, firm handshake. Americans **interpret*** this as "I'm honest. You can trust me. I can get the job done." A weak handshake seems to say "I have no energy. I can't do the job." A **limp*** handshake feels unpleasant to Americans. It's like holding a dead fish!

Here's how to shake hands: (If you have gloves on, take them off.) Reach your right hand out. **Grip*** the other person's hand firmly. Do *not* **crush***, please! Shake just once. Let go. Do *not* hold the person's hand for long. If your hands are dirty or wet, do not shake hands. Say *"Sorry, my hands are [wet]."*

Many men shake hands when they meet again in business meetings. In social meetings, however, they may just say *"Hi."*

Americans like **eye contact***. We like to feel that the other person is interested in knowing us. We feel that eye contact is a sign of honesty.

Americans often smile during an introduction. This shows that we are friendly, and glad to meet the new person.

In **formal*** situations there are special rules for introducing two people. For example: *"Mary, this is John. John, this is Mary."*

At work you would say: *"[superior*], this is [subordinate*]."* Then, say: *[subordinate], this is [superior]."*

"Mr. Thomas, this is Susan Jones, the new assistant. Ms. Jones, this is Mr. Thomas. He's the supervisor of this department."

Among equals, outside of work say *"[older person], this is [younger person]."* Or *"[female], this is [male]."*

At a school, introduce teachers and parents by their title and last name: "Ms. Claire, this is my father, *Mr. Garcia."*

In a business office, people may be introduced by first *and* last names: "Mr. Johnson, this is *Miguel Garcia."* At some work sites, male workers might use their last names only: *"Jones, this is Garcia."* At a party, people are often introduced by first names: *"This is Miguel."*

Word Help

first impression *noun phrase*. The first idea you have about a person, as soon as you meet him or her.
introduce *verb*. Tell people each other's names so they can know each other.
interpret *verb*. To give or tell the meaning of words or actions
limp *adjective*. Not firm; having no energy or strength.
grip *verb*. To hold firmly, but not tightly.
crush *verb*. To press something very hard, in order to hurt or break it.

eye contact *noun phrase*. The meeting of two people's eyes when they look at each other.
formal *adjective*. Following fixed rules for behavior or dress; behavior at important occasions.
superior *noun*. A person who is in charge of others' work
subordinant *noun*. A person who takes orders from another person.

After the introduction, a person may shake hands and say *"Hello." Or "I'm glad to know you." Or "It's nice to meet you."* The other person may say *"My pleasure."* Or *"Same here."*

The phrase *"How do you do?"* is very formal. It is not really a question. The **response*** is also *"How do you do?"*

Many people have business cards, but they do not use them in social introductions. If you later talk about business, you can ask for the other person's business card. It's OK to write notes to help you remember details of the meeting on the back of the card.

Are you the one who is making the introductions? Give some information that can help people start a conversation: *"Mr. Marcus, this is Alma Ramirez. She's the new computer technician."*

Among friends, you might say, *"Sherry, this is Alma. She's from Argentina."*

Sometimes you are among strangers in a class, at a party, or at your new job. No one introduces you. Don't worry. Introduce yourself. You can say *"Hello. My name is Alma. I'm Mr. Marcus's assistant."* Or *"Hi. My name is Alma. I'm new here."* Then ask the other person for his or her name.

If you didn't hear or remember a person's name, ask the person to repeat it: *"I'm sorry, I didn't **catch*** your name."* Or *"Can you say your name again, please?"*

How do you get started in a conversation?

Word Help

response *noun.* Answer.
catch *verb.* Hear well.

Don't worry about being interest*ing*. Be interest*ed* in the other person. "How long have you worked for this company?" "What's your job here?" "Have you always lived in New York?"

Look at the person you are talking to. Use a person's name when you talk to him or her.

Find out what the other person is good at or likes to talk about. Ask questions when you don't understand something he or she says. However, avoid personal questions. Americans usually don't ask each other their age, how much they paid for something, or how much money they earn.

It's OK to **disagree*** politely, but it's best to avoid **controversial* topics*** at a first meeting.

Don't **interrupt*** when someone else is talking. On the other hand, don't talk for too long!

If you and a friend are with people who don't understand your native language, speak to your friend in English. If you can't, then say "Excuse us, please."

Don't **whisper*** to keep another person from hearing your conversation. Don't **brag*** about yourself.

disagree *verb.* To have a different opinion about something.
controversial *adjective.* Able to cause disagreement; not universally agreed on, with strong opinions about different sides.
topic *noun.* The subject of a conversation
interrupt *verb.* To start speaking before the other person has finished speaking.
whisper *verb.* To speak very softly to someone, so others cannot hear.
brag *verb.* To speak well of oneself, telling of one's good points, accomplishments, money, etc.

Let's talk about it.

1. What is a first impression? Why is it important?

2. What is "body language?"

3. What does a strong, firm handshake seem to say to an American?

4. What does a weak, limp handshake seem to say to an American?

5. What are some things to remember when you shake someone's hand?

6. Why do Americans look at each other when they speak? How might an American feel if a person doesn't look at him or her?

7. Which names do people use during introductions in the following places:

   a. at work in an office

   b. at a party

   c. in an all-male group of workers?

Using new words:
Match the word with its meaning.

_____ 8. to press or squeeze something very hard in order to break or hurt it

_____ 9. weak, with no strength or energy

_____ 10. the idea you have about a person soon after meeting him or her

_____ 11. to change something back to the way it was before

_____ 12. to hold firmly

_____ 13. to look at someone who is looking at you

_____ 14. help people meet each other

A. first impression

B. undo

C. introduce

D. limp

E. grip

F. crush

G. make eye contact

Write a word in each sentence to make it correct. Choose from this list: yourself, repeat, one, stand, firm, meet, honesty.

15. Americans say, "You only have _____ chance to make a good first impression.

16. It's polite to _____ when you are being introduced to someone.

17. Americans like a _____ handshake.

18. Americans feel that eye contact is a sign of _____.

19. After the introduction, a person might say, "It's nice to _____ you."

20. If you are at a party and no one introduces you, introduce _____.

21. If you didn't hear a person's name, or you forgot it, ask the person to _____ it.

5. "Small Talk"

Small talk is what we say when we have nothing to say. We have a **formula*** for meaningless little conversations. This makes it easy to be with people we don't know very well.

There is nothing personal, and not much information, in small talk. It is safe. It is not **controversial***. Small talk sometimes comes before a more meaningful **conversation.*** Or, it could be the *only* communication we have with someone.

The most popular small-talk topic is our health. But we don't really tell any facts about our health.

"Hi, how are ya?" Also: *"How ya doin'?"* (*"How are you doing?"*) *"How've ya been?"* *"How's the family?"*

The answers may be: *"Fine."* *"Great."* *"**So-so***."* *"Can't **complain***."*

And, of course, you must ask the other person *"And how are you?"*

The second most popular **topic*** for small talk is the weather

"Is it hot enough for ya?"

"It sure is."

"Beautiful weather we're having, isn't it?"

"It sure is."

"It looks like rain."

"Hmm. Yeah. I think you're right."

"Nice weather for ducks." (It's raining.)

"Yeah."

"It looks like it'll clear soon."

"I hope so."

Other small-talk topics are things that have happened **recently***

"What's new?"

"Nothing much. Same old thing. What's new with you?"

"How'd you like the parade?

"It was great. My kids liked the clowns."

Students use small talk when they meet other students.

"How was the homework?"

"Really hard."

"What do you think of the teacher?
"Oh, he's all right. I'm not complaining.

"How did you do on the test?"
"I got a B."

People may also **comment*** on some news that they are sure everyone knows about. They

Word Help

formula *noun.* A set of steps for doing something; a set of rules to make something work.
controversial *adjective.* Full of ideas that people have different opinions about; causing disagreements and arguments.
conversation *noun.* People talking to each other.
so-so *adverb.* Not good, not bad.
complain *verb.* To tell something bad or wrong about something.
topic *noun.* The subject that people have a conversation about.

recently *adverb.* Not too long ago; in the past few days.
comment *verb.* To say something about; to give an opinion on something.

18

are also pretty sure the other person has the same **opinion*** as they do:

"Isn't it awful about the floods in Mississippi?"

"Oh, yes, really awful."

A co-worker or neighbor may ask about a holiday coming soon:

"Are you going to dress up for Halloween?"

"Are you having company for Thanksgiving?"

"Are you ready for Christmas?"

The answer is *"Yes"* or *"No"*—and then, *"How about you?"*

If it is near or on a holiday, people often greet each other with:

"Happy Thanksgiving!" "Happy Hanukkah" "Merry Christmas!" "Happy New Year!" "Happy Valentine's Day!" "Happy Easter!"

If we don't know a person's religion, we generally say "Happy Holidays" in late December.

Answer: *"Same to you!"*

After the holiday is past, a person may ask *"How was your Thanksgiving?" "How was your Christmas?"* Or *"How was your holiday?"*

The response is usually *"Great! How was yours?"*

Sports is a common topic among men. However, this is more than small talk! Men who like sports follow the games of their favorite

teams; they know the heroes and their **statistics***; they have seen the recent games and the exciting actions of the players.

TV used to be a common topic for small talk. Twenty years ago, there were only a few channels. Many people watched the same shows. Today, with cable TV, it's hard to find two people who watch the same shows! However, some *big* events can be topics for small talk:

"Did you watch the President's speech last night?"

"No, I missed it. I read it on the Internet later, though."

When a person wants to make friends, they go beyond small talk. They might add a bit of news to open a conversation: *"My children came over." "We went out to eat."* People with a lot of time may stop to have a longer conversation. Busy people might like to talk, but have no time. They excuse themselves: *"Well, I gotta go now . . ."* or *"I'll let you go now; I know you're busy."*

You can say good-bye in many ways:

"Bye."

"See you later." (It doesn't really mean that. It means good-bye.)

"We'll have to get together." (It doesn't mean that. It means good bye.)

"See you."

"Take care."

"Get home safe."

"Have fun!"

"Have a nice day."

Word Help

opinion *verb.* A judgement; a person's feelings or thoughts about something.

statistics *noun, plural.* The games won and lost by each team, the batting averages, runs batted in, home runs, etc. of each player.

Let's talk about it.

1. What are some "small-talk" topics?

2. Do people use "small talk" in your native country?

3. What topics do you like to talk about?

4. What topics are controversial?

5. When should you stay away from controversial topics?

Answer these "small-talk" questions with "small-talk" answers:

6. Is it hot enough for you?

7. What are you doing for the holidays?

8. Do you think it will rain?

9. Terrible weather we're having, isn't it?

10. What's new?

11. How's your family?

12. Isn't it awful about the fire at school?

13. Happy New Year!

14. How was your vacation?

15. Did you see the Yankee game last night?

16. See you later.

Using new words:
Match the word with its meaning.

_____ 17. a set or rules for doing something   A. conversation

_____ 18. taking turns speaking and listening   B controversial

_____ 19. a person's feelings or judgment about something   C. formula

_____ 20. causing people to disagree   D. topic

_____ 21. the subject of a conversation   E. comment

_____ 22. to give one's opinion about a topic   F. opinion

Write a word in each sentence to make it correct. Choose from this list: sports, nothing, health, conversation.

23. Small talk is what we say when we have _____ to say.

24. The most popular small-talk topic is _____ .

25. Many men often talk about _____

26. Small talk may come before a more meaningful

_____

6.   Smile!

When you're smiling,

When you're smiling,

The whole world smiles with you.

These are the words of a song that has been around for a long time.

Does everyone smile "in the same language"?

Most Americans think so. Americans feel that they can **communicate*** with smiles. They feel that a smile can cross any **language barrier***. But what a surprise! Smiles are *not* the same in every culture.

Most Americans smile easily at people when they meet. Americans in *some* areas of the country (outside of big cities) will smile at **total strangers*** they pass on the street. Healthy children smile very easily. Adults smile less. In general, women smile more than men.

People use smiling to make others feel welcome.

We smile to **include*** new people in a group.

We smile to show we are pleased.

Americans smile for their photographs. If a person doesn't feel like smiling, the photographer says "*Say cheese.*" When we say a word with a long *ee* sound, we have to open our mouth and show our teeth. So it looks as though we are smiling.

Americans spend a lot of money for dentists to straighten their children's teeth. One reason is so we will have "good smiles." In some other cultures, straight teeth are not important. In some cultures, people cover their teeth when they smile.

A smile can cause **misunderstandings***. People from some

Word Help

communicate *verb*. To speak or write one's ideas so another person can understand what you mean.
language barrier *noun phrase*. The wall between people who speak different languages. It stops them from communicating well.
total stranger *noun phrase*. A complete stranger. A person you have never met and never seen before.
include *verb*. To make someone a part of a group.

misunderstanding *noun*. A mistaken idea that a person gets because he or she did not understand what another person said or meant.

areas in China smile only at people they know. People from that area may think that a smiling person wants to become friends. They are confused when an American smiles, but does not become friendlier.

Japanese people smile for the same reasons Americans do. But they *also* smile when they are **embarrassed***. They may smile when they are in pain! Americans may not understand this at all.

Americans generally *look* sad when they *feel* sad. But people in some other cultures hide their sad feelings. They smile, instead. They don't want to make others feel bad. Americans may not understand this. They may think that a smiling person is *glad* that a sad thing has happened.

In big cities, it's not always safe to smile at strangers. You don't know who they are and if they are dangerous. Women may feel safe to smile at other women and children. They'll be more careful not to smile at strange men.

Americans smile at the people we see often. We smile at neighbors and people who work in the banks, Post Office, or the stores where we shop.

If someone doesn't smile back, we wonder: *Is the person angry? Too busy? Do people from this person's culture hate Americans? Is this person dangerous?*

A smile is a reward. Teachers put little "smiley face" stickers on young students' good papers. People put smiley faces in their letters to show friendly feelings. Smiley face posters are popular.

If you own a store, or if you want to sell things to Americans, learn to smile easily. It's good for business.

Smiling is also good for your health! You don't have to wait till you are happy to smile. Smile, and you'll soon be happy. The muscles that make you smile also control **glands*** in our cheeks. These glands produce a natural chemical that make us feel good.

Enjoy smiling. Enjoy other people's smiles. But remember that an American smile may not mean the same thing it means in your culture.

If you see someone here without a smile, give them one of yours!

Word Help

embarrassed *verb, past participle.* Ashamed or feeling foolish because of doing or saying something wrong.

gland *noun.* A very small body part that has the job of producing hormones, endorphins, digestive juices, etc.

Let's talk about it.

1. Does a smile mean the same thing in every language? Explain.

2. What are some reasons that Americans smile?

   Do *you* smile for these reasons?

3. Why do Americans want their children to have straight teeth?

4. What are some ways people can misunderstand a smile?

5. What does it mean when a photographer tells you to say "cheese."

Using new words:
Match the word with its meaning.

_____ 6. people who have never met

_____ 7. feeling ashamed because of a mistake

_____ 8. to make a person feel part of a group

_____ 9. When people cannot understand each
other because they speak different
languages, they have a language

_____.

_____ 10. to speak to, and listen to another person

_____ 11. When a person gets the wrong idea about
what another person said, it's a

_____.

A. communicate

B. barrier

C. total strangers

D. include

E. misunderstanding

F. embarrassed

**Write a word to make each sentence correct. Choose from this list:
communicate, teeth, welcome, language.**

12. Americans feel they can _____ with
smiles.

13. However, smiles are not the same in every _____.

14. Americans smile to make other people feel _____ to a
group.

15. In some cultures, people cover their _____ when they
smile.

25

7.   Body Language

When you learn a new language, you expect to learn many new things: new words, new sounds, new grammar, and the new "music" of speaking. In addition, there is a new *body language* to learn. The eyes, the hands, and the whole body have something to say! In a new culture, you have to understand those meanings, too.

Eyes

In *some* cultures, children are taught *not* to look directly at someone. They learn that looking directly at a person shows a **lack*** of **respect***.

It's quite different in the U.S.

Many American parents and teachers tell children, *"Look* at me when I'm talking to you!" We feel sure that the other person is listening if we can see his or her eyes. We think that it is important to **make eye contact*** during a conversation. To us, it's a sign of **openness*** and honesty. It shows respect. We think that a person who doesn't look at us may be hiding the truth.

On the other hand, we generally **avoid*** eye contact with complete strangers on the street. We may make eye contact with people in our class, club, or neighborhood. Eye contact is a sign that we are in the same group.

There are **regional*** differences, too. People on the West Coast enjoy more eye contact than people on the East Coast.

Parents teach their children not to **stare*** at strangers. Small children are curious about the world. They enjoy seeing new things and new kinds of people. They often stare at anyone who looks different. "Don't stare. It's not polite," is what their parents teach them.

Personal space

People keep a distance between themselves and the person they are speaking to.

How wide is this distance?

In the U.S., people generally stand "at **arm's length***" (about 30 inches) away from a person they are talking to. Only family members, small children, and **sweethearts*** come closer.

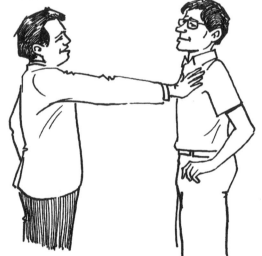

Word Help

lack *verb*. To *not* have.
respect *noun*. The show of good manners and proper admiration of a person who is superior at work or in age, official position, etc.
make eye contact *idiom*. To look at someone who is looking at you.
openness *noun*. An ability to speak directly and honestly, without hiding something.
avoid *verb*. To stay away from.

regional *adjective*. Based on the part of the country people are from.
stare *verb*. To look at someone for a long time without moving your eyes away.
arm's length *noun*. The distance from an adult's shoulder to the hand—about 30 inches.
sweethearts *noun, plural*. Two people in love with each other.

26

South Americans, southern Europeans, and Middle Eastern people stand closer to each other (22 to 26 inches). If they are speaking to an American, the American may feel uncomfortable. The American **backs away*** to his or her comfort zone. The speaker comes closer again.

On the other hand, people from Japan, China, and some northern European countries stand farther away (36 inches). To those people, Americans seem to "get too close." And to Americans, those other people seem "cold" and **distant***.

Sitting

In a social group, American women often sit with their ankles crossed, or sometimes their legs crossed at the knee. Men often sit with one leg crossing the other, with the ankle resting on the knee.

Touch

People from different cultures have very different feelings about hugging and touching. Some Americans may touch the arm of the person they are talking to while they are speaking. A man may gently slap another man on the back when **greeting*** him. Many Americans hug their family members and good friends when they greet them or say good-bye.

However, some Americans do not enjoy being hugged in public. There is a great variety of feelings about hugging strangers. Some people

will warmly hug a new person they are introduced to. Others may take take a long time before they give a friend a hug when they say hello or good-bye.

People from South America or southern Europe frequently touch the person they are speaking to. They touch on the arm, hand, or shoulder.

People from Japan **seldom*** touch at all when speaking to others.

A hug, a touch, or standing close may mean nothing special to one person. It can mean **romance*** to a second person. And it can be **offensive*** to a third person.

American **psychologists*** say that hugs are good for us: "Four hugs a day is a **minimum*** requirement for good health. Six is better, and eight is best." However, a hug from someone you don't wish to hug is *not* welcome.

If you love hugs, there are more on the West Coast than on the East Coast! Californians in general are much more "huggy" than New Yorkers.

Word Help

back away *verb phrase*. To move backward.
distant *adjective*. Having no emotional warmth; seeming not to care about another person.
greet *verb*. To say hello.

seldom *adverb*. Almost never.
romance *noun*. The beginnings of love.
offensive *adjective*. Rude; impolite; causing bad feelings.
psychologist *noun*. A person who studies human behavior or treats emotional problems.
minimum *adjective*. The smallest amount.

Let's talk about it.

1. What are some of the things you learn when you learn a new language?

2. What does *make eye contact* mean?

3. In your native culture, do people make eye contact in a conversation?

4. In your native culture, do children look at a parent or adult who is speaking to them?

5. What might *no* eye contact mean to an American?

6. Do this experiment: Stand at a comfortable distance from a classmate from your own country.

   a. What is the distance from your shoulder to the other person's shoulder?

   b. Move three inches closer. Do you feel uncomfortable? How?

7. Which national groups might want more distance from you than you want from them? Which national groups would want to be closer?

8. In your culture, do people touch others when talking to them? Do people usually hug friends when they greet them?

9. What differences have you noticed in your own eye contact, personal space, and touch since you came to the U.S.?

28

Using new words:
Match the word with its meaning.

_____ 10. about thirty inches

_____ 11. stay away from

_____ 12. the act of looking at someone who is looking at you is making ___

_____ 13. not have something

_____ 14. a person you are in love with

_____ 15. look at for a long time

_____ 16. a feeling of admiration and appreciation

_____ 17. almost never

A. lack

B. respect

C. eye contact

D. avoid

F. seldom

G. stare

I. arm's length

J. sweetheart

Write a word to make the sentence correct. Choose from these words: arm's, hug, eye contact, look, polite.

18. Many parents say to their children: " _____ at me when I am talking to you."

19. Don't stare at that man. It's not _____.

20. In the U.S., people generally stand at _____ length away from a person they are speaking with.

21. Americans often make _____ while they are having a conversation with someone.

22. Many Americans _____ their friends and members of their family when they greet them.

8. Manners Around Doors

Americans have many manners and **customs*** about doors. Our door manners seem **mysterious*** to people from Japan and other Asian countries. That's because our doors are made differently. American doors are hung on **hinges***. The hinges let the doors swing out or in. In many Asian homes and stores, doors open by sliding *sideways* into the wall.

Public Doors

It's good manners to hold a door open for the person behind you. Make sure a door doesn't close when another person is coming near the doorway.

Traditionally*, a man opens a door for a woman, and allows her to go through the doorway first. This is no longer a firm custom among younger people. Young men and young women are "equal" before the door. It does not matter who holds the door. However, on a **date***, a girl might slow down and let the boy get to the door first. The boy can show his traditional manners and open the door for her.

When two or more people are walking toward a door, the first person to reach it should open it. He or she may then hold the door open and let the second person go through the doorway.

Or, the first person goes through the door and "passes" the open door to the next person. If someone accidentally lets a door close as another person is walking to it, he or she says, "*Oh, I'm sorry.*"

If a person holds a door for you, say, "*Thank you.*" The other person should say, "*You're welcome*" or "*No problem*" —but there is no need to say anything at all.

If two people reach the door at the exact same time, the "stronger" person opens the door and allows the "weaker" person to go first. That is, we hold the door open for a person carrying packages, for a mother with a child, for a **disabled*** or **elderly*** person. Also, we hold the door for our parent, teacher, or any older person, to show **respect***.

The person that the door is held for may say, "*Thank you.*" If the door is a really heavy one , a weak person may ask a stronger person to open it first.

If you are carrying packages or pushing a stroller, you can ask someone to help: "*Could you please open the door for me?*"

Word Help

custom *noun*. An activity that has been done for a long time in the same way.
mysterious *adjective*. Like a mystery; hard to understand
hinge *noun*. A small device that holds a door to the door frame, and allows the door to swing.
traditionally *adverb*. According to the way it was done in the past.
date *noun*. A meeting at a set time to do something with a boyfriend or girlfriend.

disabled *adjective*. Not able to fully use ones arms, legs, eyes, etc.
elderly *adjective*. Old
respect *noun*. The showing of honor or caring for another person.

Elevator doors

Traditionally, men let women get off an elevator first, and held the door open. Today, whoever is nearest the door gets off first. Generally, people in an elevator cooperate to make sure all elderly people, disabled people, or people with **bundles*** or baby **strollers*** get out safely.

Bus and Subway Doors

Are you waiting for a bus or a subway? When it comes and the doors open, *stand out of the way!* Let the people inside the bus or train get off before you try to get on it. (It's not just good manners—it's good sense. Everyone will get on faster.)

Private Doors

Years ago, almost everyone kept their doors at home open. They expected neighbors and friends to walk right in. Not today! In many places, Americans worry about robbers entering their homes. They usually lock their doors. Many doors in cities have "peepholes." You can look through the hole to see who is knocking at your door before you open it.

It is **rude*** to walk into someone's home, even if the door is open. You should knock on the door, or ring the doorbell, or **announce*** that you are at the door. Wait for an invitation to enter.

Sometimes, when a family is having a party, they may leave the door open so latecomers can come in. In that case, you can ring the doorbell and walk in. That will let your host know that someone else has arrived.

A guest may usually go into in the living room, dining room, and kitchen. He or she doesn't usually enter other rooms in the house unless invited. A guest asks permission to use the bathroom: **"May I use your bathroom?"**

Door conversations

A woman hears a knock on her door.

"Who is it?" she asks.

"It's me, Mary Ann."

"Oh, please come in." Or, if the door is locked, *"Just a minute."*

Or *"Hi, come on in."* The woman opens the door and *stands aside* to allow the guest to walk in.

Sometimes the person at home is busy, or does not want to invite the other person in. He or she may stand in the doorway and **chat***.

Word Help

bundle *noun*. A package that someone is carrying.
stroller *noun*. A small carriage in which a child rides, sitting up.
rude *adjective*. Having bad manners; not polite.
announce *verb*. 1. Give information. 2. Speak in a strong voice.

chat *verb*. To have a pleasant conversation about topics that are not very serious.

Let's talk about it.

1. Are there differences between doors in your native country and doors in the United States?

2. Are there special manners around doors in your native country? Tell about them.

3. When should you hold the door open for others?

4. What are elevator-door manners in your native country?

5. What manners have you noticed in elevators in the U.S.?

6. Why do most Americans keep their doors locked?

7. Is it necessary to lock your door in your native city? Why, or why not?

8. What should you do if you go to visit friends and their door is open?

Using new words:
Match the word with its meaning.

_____ 9. old

_____ 10. to publicly or officially tell someone something

_____ 11 These hold doors to a frame so the doors can swing open.

_____ 12. bad-mannered; not polite

_____ 13. unknown; hard to understand

_____ 14. a traditional way of doing something

_____ 15. package

_____ 16. to honor, admire, and treat well

_____ 17. not able to use legs or arms properly

A. mysterious

B. elderly

C. bundle

D. custom

E. hinges

F. disabled

G. respect

H. rude

I. announce

Write a word to make the sentences correct. Choose from this list: rude, nearest, I'm sorry, behind, mysterious, off.

18. Our door manners seem _____ to people from Japan and other Asian countries.

19. It's good manners to hold a door open for the person _____ you.

20. If you accidentally let a door close as another person is coming to the door, say "_____."

21. Whoever is _____ the door of an elevator gets off first.

22. Let the people who are on a bus get _____ the bus before you get on it.

23. It's _____ to walk into a house without knocking.

Do you have a cold? Is your nose **running***? Go ahead and **blow your nose***! Don't just sit there and **sniff***!

In some countries, doctors tell people not to blow their nose. It's bad for their ears! In other countries, it is bad manners to blow your nose in front of other people.

However, in the U.S. it is bad manners to **sniffle*** when your nose is running.

Carry tissues with you. Use them. Someone may **offer*** you a tissue. Take it. Turn your head away from people when you blow your nose. Say "Excuse me," before you blow your nose. Blow quietly, please. Don't blow your nose at a table when people are eating. It's better to leave the table. Throw the tissue away when you are through. Wash your hands.

It's good manners to cover your mouth

when you cough. Then say "*Excuse me.*" Cover your mouth with a tissue or handkerchief. People don't want to spread **germs***.

It's bad manners to **yawn*** while talking to someone. Cover your mouth, and say "I'm sorry." Offer a reason—"It's not the conversation—I didn't get enough sleep last night."

But many Americans don't usually say "*Excuse me*" when they sneeze. Most often, someone near them will say "*Bless* you.*"

Why?

Saying "God bless you" or "Bless you" is a very old **custom***. Most Americans do not know why people do this. It's just good manners today.

The reason people say "God bless you" is this: hundreds of years ago, people thought these words could save their lives!

In the Christian religion, Satan (the Devil) is

Word Help

run *verb*. To drip liquid or mucous. "The baby has a runny nose." "My nose is running."
blow (your nose) *verb phrase*. To close your mouth and blow mucous out of your nose and into a handkerchief or tissue (not into your fingers, please!)
sniff *verb*. To take a short, small breath in order to keep your nose from dripping or running when you have a cold.
sniffle *verb*. To make sniffing sounds when a nose is running; to cry quietly.
offer *verb*. To ask if someone wants something.

germs *noun, plural*. Bacteria that cause illness.
yawn. *verb*. To open the mouth widely to get more air into the lungs when one is sleepy.
bless *verb*. To give God's help and protection
custom *noun*. A way of doing something that has been done that way for a long time.

responsible for many of the bad things in the world. Christians had fears that Satan could enter a person's body and "**possess***" the person. If the Devil got someone's **soul***, that person would not be able to go to Heaven.

People felt that Satan was always looking for an easy way to get into a person. When a person sneezed, there was a moment of **weakness***. A person could not protect himself or herself during a sneeze. He or she needed God's help, or blessing.

In the 1400s there was a terrible illness going through Europe. It was called "The Black Death." One-fourth of the population of Europe died from it. A sneeze was one of the first **symptoms***. People got into the habit of saying "God bless you!" to protect each other.

People do not think of this anymore. A sneeze does not mean there is danger of dying or of being possessed by the Devil. But the custom is a very strong one! So, when someone sneezes, someone nearby will say "*God bless you.*" They say it even if they do not know the person. The sneezer says "*Thank you.*"

People who are not Christian may say simply, "*Bless you.*" You may also hear people saying "***Gesundheit****" when someone sneezes. This is the German word for "Good health."

Some people think it is **silly*** to say "*God bless you.*" They say that a sneeze is just like a cough. They say that a sneezer should say "*Excuse me.*" But others may still say, "*God bless you*" to the sneezer. You never know which of these people is near you. Be on the safe side: say "Excuse me," when you sneeze. And if the other person sneezes, say "Bless you."

Smoking

Fewer than 25% of adult Americans smoke. Smoking is not allowed at schools, at workplaces, in public transportation, or in public buildings.

Many people (even smokers) are aware of the dangers of **second-hand smoke***. They do not **allow*** smoking in their homes. Be prepared to smoke outside. Bring your own ashtray. Do not leave cigarette **ashes*** or **butts*** on the ground. If you smoke, shake out your coat or jacket before you enter someone's home. *You* can't smell the smoke in your clothes, but a nonsmoker *can*.

Word Help

weakness *noun*. A condition of having no strength or power.
possess *verb*. To take over as one's own property.
soul *noun*. The spirit part of a person that lives on after death.
symptom *noun*. A sign of a sickness: fever, sneezing, rash, etc.

gesundheit! [guh zunt' hiyt] *noun*. A German word that means "good health to you!"
silly *adjective*. Foolish, not good sense.
second-hand smoke *noun phrase*. Smoke from another person, not oneself. 4,000 Americans die each year from second-hand smoke, so it is not popular!
allow *verb*. To let; to give permission.
butt *noun, slang*. The part of a cigarette that is left when a person cannot smoke it anymore.
ashes *noun, plural*. A soft, light gray powder left from something that has burned.

Let's talk about it.

1. What are some good manners about blowing your nose?

2. Are these the same manners in your native country? Tell about them.

3. What are some good manners when you cough?

4. What are good manners when you sneeze? When someone else sneezes?

5. How did the custom of saying "God bless you!" begin?

6. If you are not Christian, what can you say when someone sneezes?

7. Tell your opinion of the custom of saying "Bless you!" or "God bless you!"

Using new words:
Match the word with its meaning.

_____ 8. the spirit of a person that continues to live after the person dies

_____ 9. the Devil

_____ 10. to make a sound by breathing air quickly into your nose

_____ 11. to say that one will give something if the other person wants it

_____ 12. a German word for *good health*

_____ 13. a sign of an illness

A. sniff

B. offer

C. soul

D. Satan

E. symptom

F. gesundheit

Write a word to make correct sentences. Choose from this list:
God bless you; cover; silly; blow; running; excuse me; eating; symptoms.

14. In some countries it is bad manners to _____ your nose in front of other people.

15. However, in the United States, it is bad manners to sniffle when your nose is _____.

16. Say _____ before you blow your nose.

17. Don't blow your nose at a table when people are _____.

18. It's good manners to _____ your mouth when you cough.

19. Many Americans don't say "Excuse me" when they sneeze. They expect someone to say "_____."

20. In the 1400s, a sneeze was one of the first _____ of the Black Death.

21. Some people think it is _____ to say "God bless you!" when someone sneezes.

37

Are you going to have dinner with Americans? That's great. Don't be nervous—just enjoy it!

Some American **table manners*** may be different from manners in your native country. It's a good time to learn about these manners. Just ask questions. It makes good dinner conversation. Your American **hosts*** will be happy to explain things. [Host – male; hostess = female]

When you are invited to someone's home for dinner, it's **customary*** to ask *"What can I bring?"* The host may say *"Oh, nothing at all; just bring yourself."* You may offer to bring a salad, a dessert, or the wine or other **beverage***. Even if the answer is no, you can still bring a small gift such as flowers, wine, or a small box of candy for the hostess. It's called a hostess gift.

The company and the conversation are usually more important than the food. So just have a good time. Relax, and be interested in what's going on.

Ask "Where would you like me to sit?" Usually the **head** and **foot of the table*** are for the hosts.

Word Help

table manners *noun, plural*. The way people speak and act while eating.
host, hostess *noun*. The person who invited you to the meal. A hostess is a woman. A host can be a man or woman.
customary *adverb*. Usual, commonly done.
beverage *noun*. Something to drink: water, milk, juice, soda, beer, wine.
head and foot [of the table] *noun*. On a rectangular table, the two opposite short sides.

Dinner may come in "courses" or parts. A "five-course" meal is an **appetizer***, soup, salad, the **entrée*** (main course), dessert, and coffee or tea. Water, milk, soda, or wine may be served with the meal.

A main course can be meat and vegetables, a **pasta*** dish, or a **casserole***. At a large wedding or elaborate party, there may be more courses. Pasta might be served before the entree. If you're not sure, ask "Is this the main course?" You don't want to eat too much appetizer before the main course comes.

At dinner in an American home, food is often brought to the table on large serving plates. Use a serving fork or spoon (not your own fork) to put some of each food on your plate. If you think you may *not* like something, take a small amount.

Don't wait for someone to **offer*** the food three times! "Would you like some potatoes?" If the answer is yes, say "Yes, please." The host will think you don't want the food if you say "No, thank you," If you don't eat, the host will think you don't like the food.

Someone may pass the serving plates around the table. Hold the plate, put some of the food on your plate, and pass the plate on to the

appetizer *noun*. A small amount of food that you eat before the main meal.
entrée *noun*. The main course of the meal.
pasta *noun*. a form of spaghetti or macaroni, ziti, etc.
casserole *noun*. A meal with rice or pasta, meat, vegetables, and sauce that is prepared in one large pot or pan and baked in the oven.
offer *verb*. To ask if someone wants something.

person next to you. If you need something that is not close to you, ask a person near it to pass it: *"Jack, could you please pass the salt?"*

When there are many guests, the hosts may serve the food **buffet style***. Then, a large table has plates with all the different foods on it. You take an empty plate, and you can help yourself. Take a napkin and **cutlery***. Then take your plate back to your seat.

Don't start to eat yet. That can seem **rude***. Wait until everyone is served, and wait until the hosts are seated. Sometimes the host or hostess will say *"Don't wait for me, start to eat"* (or ***"Dig right in***"). In that case, watch what others do, and follow their example.

In some families, there is a short **prayer*** before people begin to eat. In a Christian family, this is called "**Grace***." Grace can be very short. The general meaning is this: *"Dear God, we thank you for the food."* One person says Grace. Everyone **bows their heads*** and closes their eyes. The grace sayer ends the prayer with the word "**Amen***."

Word Help

buffet [buh fay'] **style** *adverb. Self-serve, with plates of food all on one table. Guests line up, take a plate, and help themselves to the things they want.*
cutlery *noun.* Knives, forks, and spoons.
rude *adjective.* Not polite; bad-mannered.
dig right in *Idiom, slang.* Start eating.
prayer *noun.* A conversation with God.
Grace *noun.* A prayer of thanks to God
bow their heads *verb phrase.* To look down, and have one's head turned down.
Amen *noun.* A word used after a prayer. It means "May it be true."

Americans eat with a knife and fork. Right-handed Americans pick up a fork with our left hand. We hold the knife in our right hand. We hold the meat down with the fork (the back side of the fork is up). We cut one piece of meat with the knife. We *don't* cut all the meat at once.

Then we place the knife down on the side of the plate. We **switch*** the fork to the right hand. We eat the piece of meat. Then we switch the fork back to the left hand, and we cut another piece. This feels like the "natural way." (Adults cut a child's meat all at once, however. Left-handed people cut with the knife in the left hand, and the fork in the right hand.) We don't use the knife to push food onto the fork.

Americans eat soup with a soup spoon. It's good manners to spoon the soup away from the near side of the bowl, not toward us. We don't "**slurp***" or make noises when we eat our soup. We eat it quietly. We don't bring the bowl to our mouth to drink the soup when we are with company. It would seem very strange. If it is a clear soup served in a cup, it is sometimes OK to drink it from the cup. Watch to see what your host or hostess does.

Americans break bread. That means, if you have a slice of bread or a roll, break it, butter one piece, and eat that piece. Then butter the next piece, and eat that.

There are some foods Americans sometimes eat with their fingers. These can be sandwiches, pizza, corn on the cob, chicken legs, and french fries. Watch the other people at the table, and do as they do. If everyone is using a fork, then use a fork. Don't lick your fingers at the table. Wipe them with your napkin.

switch *verb.* To change or move.
slurp *verb.* To make a sucking sound while drinking or eating soup.

Let's talk about it.

1. You are invited to a dinner party. What can you offer to bring?

2. What is a hostess gift?

3. What are the parts of a "five-course meal"?

4. What does "Help yourself!" mean?

5. Someone passes a serving plate to you. What do you do?

6. What is a buffet-style dinner?

7. When is it good manners to start to eat?

8. What is Grace?

9. In your native country, do people say anything special before eating?

10. How do Americans cut and eat meat?

11. How do *you* usually cut your meat?

12. What are some manners about eating soup?

13. What foods do Americans eat with their fingers?

14. Have you been invited to an American dinner party? Tell about it.

15. What are your favorite foods?

40

Using new words:
Match the word with its meaning.

_____ 16. the person who invites others to his or her home, or to a party

_____ 17. thin pieces of wood used by many Asians for eating

_____ 18. to make a noise when eating or drinking a liquid

_____ 19. a word at the end of a prayer: "May it be so."

_____ 20. "Please start to eat." (slang)

_____ 21. to exchange the places of two things

_____ 22. the first part of a meal

_____ 23. the main part of a meal

_____ 24. polite customs people follow when eating together

_____ 25. a prayer of thanks to God

A. chopsticks

B. table manners

C. Grace

D. appetizer

E. entrée

F. switch

G. Amen

H. slurp

I. host

J. "Dig right in."

11.

Table Manners, Part II

Americans have a standard way to set a table. The dinner plate is in the center. A knife is on the right. (The sharp edge faces the plate.) A teaspoon is to the right of the knife. If there will be soup, the soup spoon is to the right of the teaspoon.

A fork is to the left of the plate. If there is salad, a salad fork will be to the left of the dinner fork. A **formal dinner*** may have a special fork for **dessert***. The dessert fork may be above the plate rather than to the side of the plate.

A **napkin*** is usually placed to the left of the plate. (The forks may be on top of the napkin.)

A water glass is above the knife. There may be a bread plate there, too.

A salad bowl may be on the dinner plate, or to the left of the fork.

When you sit down to a **meal***, don't put things on the table. Put your handbag, sun glasses, keys, etc. someplace else. take the napkin and place it on your **lap***. The napkin is usually kept folded in half. If your mouth gets wet or **greasy***, use the napkin to **wipe*** it. You can also use the napkin to clean up anything that drips. In an emergency, like spilled water, put your napkin on it quickly.

It's polite to **compliment*** the **host*** or **hostess*** for the meal. *"Mmmm, this is delicious."* Other comments: *"I love the sauce. What's your secret?" "How do you make it?" "May I have the recipe?"*

If the host asks *"How do you like the squash?"* (and squash is something you *don't* like*), don't* say that you like it. (The host may put more on your plate!) Just say *"Mmmm the squash. I never tasted it before. It has an . . . uh. . . interesting taste."*

If the host asks, *"Would you like more?"*

Say, *"No, thank you."*

Or *"Yes, please."*

Word Help

formal dinner *noun phrase*. A meal that has some fixed rules about the way food is cooked and served, the order of serving, and manners. People dress in good clothes, and use their "best manners."

dessert *noun*. A sweet food eaten at the end of a meal: ice cream, cake, pie, fruit, etc.

napkin *noun*. A large square of paper or cloth used to protect your clothing when you are eating, and to wipe your hands and mouth.

meal *noun*. Breakfast, lunch, or dinner; an amount of food that will keep a person from being hungry for a few hours.

lap *noun*. The flat area formed by one's upper legs, when you sit down.

greasy *adjective*. Oily, from the fat of meat or butter.

wipe *verb*. To make a motion to clean something.

compliment 1. *verb*. To say something nice. 2. *noun*. Words that tell a person he or she is good in some way.

host, hostess *noun*. The person who invited you to the meal. A *hostess* is a woman. A *host* now means a man *or* woman.

Chew your food with your mouth closed. *Never* talk with food in your mouth.

Wait until everyone has had a first serving before you ask for a **second helping***.

At a **formal dinner***, let one hand rest in your lap (except when you are cutting your meat) while you hold the fork and eat with the other hand. Don't rest your elbows on the table.

Please don't **burp*** to show you like the food. Americans think that a burp is an **unpleasant*** sound. If you must let air out of your stomach, keep it quiet. Cover your mouth and say *"Excuse me."*

If there is something in your mouth (such as a small bone) that you cannot **swallow***, do this: Hide your mouth with your napkin with your left hand. Remove the object from your mouth with your right hand. Place the object on your plate. Do not **mention*** it or call attention to it. If you must leave the table during the meal, quietly say *"Excuse me, please"* as you get up.

Don't blow your nose while people are eating. Leave the table, or turn away from the table. Don't pick your teeth clean at the table. Don't eat too quickly or too slowly. Don't lean your chair back on two legs. Don't drink too much alcohol and become **silly***.

If you have a cell phone, turn the ringer off. Don't answer the cell phone while you are at the table. Excuse yourself if you must answer an important call. Leave the table, and speak in another room. Do not hold a conversation, but return to the table as quickly as possible. Say, *"I'm very sorry. It was an important call I had to take."*

Avoid* conversations about unpleasant things. Don't talk about illness, bathroom topics, accidents or death at the dinner table. Avoid **strong opinions***, too. Dinner conversation should be about *pleasant* things, to help the **digestion***!

It's OK to leave food on your plate if you don't want to eat it. (Avoid giving yourself too much food!) When you are finished eating, put your knife and fork on your plate. Do not put them on the table. Don't leave them in bowls or cups.

Should you help clear the table or wash the dishes? It's polite to **offer*** to help. *("Can I help with the dishes?")* The host may say, "No, you're the guest," to a first-time guest. But you have become "one of the family" when the host or hostess lets you help clear the table, or do other cleanup work.

If the host or hostess does not smoke, do not smoke at the table. Many American homes are "smoke-free." Guests smoke outdoors, if they have to. (Don't leave cigarette butts or ashes on your host's ground outside.)

Word Help

second helping *noun*. Another portion of food.
burp *verb*. To allow air from your stomach to come up noisily through your mouth.
unpleasant *adjective*. Not good; causing a bad feeling.
swallow *verb*. To move food from the mouth down into the stomach.
mention *verb*. To include something in a conversation.

silly *adjective* Foolish; behaving stupidly.
avoid *verb*. To stay away from.
strong opinions *noun, plural*. Ideas that you hold very strongly and that might disagree with the opinions of others.
digestion. *noun*. The process [in the stomach and intestines] of turning food into usuable materials for your body.
offer *verb*. To ask if someone would like something.

Let's talk about it.

1. Americans set the table with the dinner plate in the center. Tell where these things are:

   a. the knife

   b. the fork

   c. the soup spoon

   d. the napkin

   e. the water glass

   f. the salad bowl

   g. the bread plate

2. What are some manners about the dinner napkin?

3. How will you compliment your host when you like the dinner?

4. What can you say if you don't like the taste of something?

5. What are some manners about chewing your food?

6. What are some manners about your hands and arms at a dinner table?

7. What can you say if you burp?

8. How can you take a small bone out of your mouth?

9. What are some manners about cell phones at the table?

10. What are some topics to avoid in conversation?

11. What does it mean if the host lets you clean the table?

Using new words:

Match the word with its meaning.

_____ 12. to stay away from

_____ 13. a cloth or soft paper. It's used during meals to protect your lap or to wipe your mouth

_____ 14. a noise made from air in the stomach as it comes up into the mouth

_____ 15. a meal when people act on their best behavior

_____ 16. the top part of your legs when you are seated

_____ 17. There is a _____ to the right of the plate. The sharp side is close to the plate.

_____ 18. not nice

_____ 19. to say something nice about a person, or the person's dress, home, work, etc.

_____ 20. to say a few words about a topic or person during a conversation or speech

_____ 21. the person who invited you to share a meal

A. burp

B. napkin

C. knife

D. unpleasant

E. formal dinner

F. avoid

G. compliment

H. host

I. mention

J. lap

Write a word to make correct sentences. Choose from this list: family, unpleasant, compliment, help.

22. It is polite to _____ the host or hostess about the meal.

23. At the dinner table, avoid conversations about _____ things.

24. It's polite to offer to _____ the host clear the table or wash the dishes.

25. A host might let you help with clean up. This is not an insult. It means you are accepted as "one of the _____."

12. Restaurant Manners

Good restaurants are often very busy on the weekends and on holidays. You may need to **make a reservation*** to be sure you can get a table. Call the restaurant one or two hours before you plan to arrive. Tell them how many people will be in your **party***. (For some holidays, you may need to call weeks in advance!)

Spell your name. *"My name is Chen, C-H-E-N. I would like to make reservations for a party of two at seven p.m."*

If you are *not* going to keep your reservation, call the restaurant to **cancel*** it. Otherwise, arrive at the time you said. A restaurant may give your table to other customers if you are not there on time. When you arrive, give your name to the **host*** right away.

Restaurants welcome **well-mannered*** children. Talk to your children about good manners in a restaurant before you go. (For example, tell them that they may not run around, or talk loud, or **disturb*** other people.) Never hit or loudly **scold*** your children in the

restaurant. Quietly take your child or children out of the dining room to solve their problem. It's a good idea to bring crayons and paper to keep a child busy and happy while you are waiting for your meal.

When you arrive in a restaurant, you may have to wait for the restaurant's host or hostess to seat you. He or she may ask *"Smoking or nonsmoking?"* If the whole restaurant is nonsmoking, smoke outside the restaurant.

If you do not have a reservation, there may be a line of customers waiting to be seated. If there is a host taking names, give your name and the number of people in your party. Then go to the end of the line, or wait in the waiting area.

When the table is ready for you, the host (or *maitre d'**) will call your name. He or she will lead you to your table. Women should follow the host, and the men follow the women. The host holds the chair for each woman. If there is no host, a gentleman may hold the chair to make it easier for a woman to sit.

If you don't like the location of your table, you can ask the host to seat you someplace else: *"May we have a table by the window?"*

The host is not the same person as your **server*** or waiter. In an expensive restaurant, there will be a server for drinks from the bar, and a different server for the meal.

Word Help

make a reservation *verb phrase*. Call in advance to ask a restaurant to reserve (save) a table for you at a certain time.
party *noun*. A group that is traveling, eating, or doing some other activity together.
cancel *verb*. Stop something from happening.
host, hostess The person who greets people at a restaurant. A hostess is female. A host can be male *or* female.
well-mannered *adjective*. Having good behavior; able to sit quietly, and speak politely.
disturb *verb*. To make noises or do things that will annoy people.
scold *verb*. To talk angrily to a child to correct bad behavior.

maitre d' [mae/ truh dee/] *noun*. A person who greets people in an expensive restaurant, and leads them to a table.
server, waiter, waitress *noun*. A person who serves food. The word *waitress* means a woman. The word *waiter* used to mean male, but now means either male or female.

"Would you like anything from the bar?"

"Yes, a glass of red wine, please—and Sprite."

Look at your menu and decide what you want to eat. You can ask your food server to explain any words you don't understand. If someone else is paying the bill, choose foods that are not very expensive.

Traditionally,* the server asks the women for their order first. Or, a woman tells her **escort*** what she wants. Then *he* tells the waiter her order. *("The lady will have the salmon steak. I will have the roast beef.")* However, nowadays, people usually order for themselves.

Wait until everyone at your table has been served. Then eat.

When you want to call the server, say, *"Waiter"* or *"Excuse me."* Try to get your server's attention by looking at him or her. It is **rude*** to whistle, shout, or snap your fingers at the server. You may wave slightly.

Sometimes there is too much food for you to eat. You can ask the server to wrap up part of it for you to take home. You might say, *"Can you wrap this up for me, please?"* Or *"I'd like a 'doggy bag*' please."*

When a group of people go to a Chinese restaurant, they usually each order one meal, and then everyone shares the different foods.

When you have finished the meal, the server will ask for dessert and coffee orders. When you have finished eating, you can signal the waiter by a small writing motion that you are ready for the check. Or say *"Our check*, please."*

The person who invited the guests is usually the person who will pay the bill, but not always. If someone does not clearly say that he or she is **treating***, pay your part of the bill. It is usual for the person who will pay the bill to check it, to be sure it is correct.

If you and your dinner partners have agreed to **"go dutch*,"** ask the server for *separate checks* before you order. In a large group, the check is often divided equally among all the diners.

Don't forget to **tip***! The usual tip is between 15% and 20% of the bill (before the tax). After you get your change from paying the bill, leave the tip on the table. If you are paying with a credit card, you can **charge*** the tip as well.

doggy bag *noun phrase, slang.* A container you take home that contains food you were not able to finish at the restaurant. It is not for your dog, it's for you to eat later.
check *noun.* A bill for the cost of dinner.
treat* *verb.* To pay for someone else's dinner or other entertainment.
go dutch *idiom.* Each person in a group pays for his or her own cost.
tip *verb.* To give the server 15% or 20% of the check, to pay for his or her service.
charge *verb.* To pay a bill by credit card.

Word Help

traditionally *adverb.* In the way it was done years ago.
escort *noun.* A leader of a group; a man accompanying a woman.
rude [rood] *adjective.* Having bad manners.

Let's talk about it.

1. When is it necessary to have reservations at a restaurant?

2. What should you do if you cannot keep your reservation?

3. How can you get your server's attention?

4. What are good manners if you bring children to a good restaurant?

5. You like your dinner, but you can't finish it all. What can you ask for?

6. Who pays the bill at the restaurant?

7. What does it mean to "go Dutch"?

8. What are some manners about tipping?

9. Have you eaten in an American restaurant? Tell about it.

10. How are American restaurant manners different from manners in your native country?

Using new words:
Match the word with its meaning.

_____ 11. The person who takes you to your table at
a restaurant

_____ 12. The person who serves your food

_____ 13. When you ask the restaurant to hold a table
for you, you are making a _____

_____ 14. group; "There will be six people in our
_____ at the restaurant

_____ 15. To tell someone that you will not keep an
appointment or a reservation.

_____ 16. to pay for someone's dinner or lunch.

_____ 17. a person who acts as a protector or guide,

A. escort

B. server or waiter

C. cancel

D. host or maitre d'

E. party

F. reservation

G. treat

Write a word in each sentence to make it correct. Choose from this list: tip, busy, non-smoking, rude, pay.

18. Good restaurants are often very _____ on weekends and
holidays.

19. Restaurants may have smoking and _____ areas.

20. It is _____ to call your waiter by whistling or snapping
your fingers, so don't do that.

20. The person who invited the other is usually the person who will
_____ for the dinner, but not always.

21. The _____ is between 15% and 20% of the bill.

13. Manners Between Men and Women

Immigrants often get confused about manners between men and women in the U.S. (That's OK. So do Americans!)

Different groups of people, and different **generations***, have different **values***. They have different standards for good manners between men and women. Manners between men and women at *social* events are different from manners at *business* events.

Many **traditional*** American manners **have their roots*** in **chivalry***. Chivalry was a set of customs that began the upper classes in Europe in the 1400s. **Knights*** had a **code of behavior***. They were supposed to be helpful to weaker people, such as children, old people and women. Each knight had a "fair

lady" he loved. He did his **brave deeds*** to honor her.

Women were "**put on a pedestal***." Men thought that women were **fragile***. (Women believed this, too.) A woman needed a man's protection in a dangerous world. A "nice woman" did not go to public places alone. She needed an **escort***.

The manners of chivalry spread from the noble class to other classes. The word *gentleman* used to mean "nobleman or landowner." Later it began to mean "a man with good manners." *Lady* meant the wife of a lord, or landowner. *Lady* later meant "a woman with good manners."

Gentlemen treated women with **respect*** in many ways. Men helped women put on their coats. Men carried heavy packages and opened doors for women. Men stood up when a woman entered the room. They allowed women to go through doors, get off elevators, and enter rooms first. Men gave up their seats on buses and subways to women. Men helped women across the street. Men took off their hats when a woman

Word Help

generation *noun*. A set of people who were born around the same time. *My grandmother's generation believed that women should not vote.*

value *noun*. Something that a person considers to have importance or worth.

traditional *adjective*. According to the way things have been done for a long time.

have their roots *verb phrase*. Began in some early form.

chivalry [shi′ vuhl ree] *noun*. A system of manners in which men are helpful to women and weaker people.

knight *noun*. In the 1300s and 1400s, a soldier of the upper class. When in battle, he wore armor and rode on horseback.

code of behavior *noun phrase*. A set of rules to guide a person's actions.

brave deeds *noun phrase*. Courageous acts; good works.

put on a pedestal *idiom*. To treat like a beautiful statue.

fragile *adjective*. Delicate; easily hurt or broken.

escort *noun*. A man who accompanies a woman to a party, restaurant, or any public place.

respect 1. *noun*. The showing of good manners or kindness toward someone. 2. *verb*. To treat carefully; to be courteous to.

was near. Men paid the bills during **courtship***
and after the marriage.

The principle of "ladies first" was taught to little
boys from the age of three or four. That meant that girls
and women had the **privileges*** of being served first,
going through doors first, and being the first to receive
things. Boys were also taught to protect and respect
girls. Boys were taught to use polite language when
girls, women, and older people were around.

In times of danger, "Save the women and
children first" was the rule. Men
enjoyed "coming to the rescue of
a **damsel in distress***." Young
women hoped to meet and marry
"**a knight in shining armor**." It
was a very **romantic*** idea.

In the 1960s, women began to
ask for **equal rights***. Young
women said that they did not want
chivalry from men. They wanted
rights. They wanted equal education
and equal career opportunities. They
wanted to be doctors, lawyers,
engineers, bus drivers, or fire fighters.
They wanted equal pay for equal
work. They said they could open their
own doors, put on their *own* coats, and pay their *own*
way on a date.

Word Help

courtship *noun*. The time when a man and women get
to know each other, to see if they want to get married.
privilege *noun*. A favor or advantage or right, that
one person or group has, that is not given to others.
A person may have a privilege because of his or her
age, money, sex, or job.
damsel in distress *noun phrase*. A young woman who
needs someone to rescue her from danger or trouble.
knight in shining armor *noun phrase*. A man who will
take care of all the problems.
romantic *adjective*. Exciting; adventurous in love.
equal rights *noun, plural*. The rights to get an
education, study any subject, do any kind of work,
and earn equal pay for equal work.

For a number of years, there was a lot of
tension* over manners. A man with traditional
good manners was confused when a woman
did not want him to pay for dinner! Women
actually got angry when men opened car doors
for them.

People over 60 are comfortable with
traditional manners and chivalry. Americans
under 60 are less **predictable***.

For many people, "chivalry is dead."
Others say that "chivalry has changed:
manners between men and women
should be equal." Men and women
should help each other. Men and
women should take turns paying for a
date. The first person to get to a door
should open it and hold it for the next
person. The person nearest the elevator
door should get off first. People should
help each other carry heavy bundles.
Both men and women should do
housework and take care of the
children. A woman could help a man on
with his coat sometimes.

Americans don't agree about
chivalry. Newcomers need to know
that both systems still **exist***. Learn
how to be chivalrous and to receive chivalry
gracefully. Also know how to treat another
person with full equality.

Today, women do not have special "ladies
first" privileges. But they do have more rights
and opportunities. Men have more rights, too!

tension *noun*. A feeling of stress because of
differences of opinion, or anger about a matter.
predictable *adjective*. It can be easy to guess what
a predictable person will say or do.
exist *verb*. Be; have life.

Let's talk about it.

1. Why do Americans get confused about manners between men and women?

2. What is chivalry?

3. How were women treated under the rules of chivalry?

4. Why did women stop enjoying privileges of chivalry?

5. Do men do special favors for women in your country, such as open doors for them, or help them on with a coat?

6. What is a "damsel in distress?"

7. What is a "knight in shining armor"?

8. Why is there tension over manners between men and women?

9. Which parts of chivalry do you like?

10. Which parts of chivalry do you *not* like?

11. Have manners between men and women been changing in your native country?

Using new words:
Match the word with its meaning.

_____ 12. delicate; easily hurt or broken

_____ 13. have a beginning

_____ 14. having the same opportunities for careers, voting, and earning money

_____ 15. a woman who needs help

_____ 16. a group of people about the same age

_____ 17. the practice of men protecting and honoring women

_____ 18. having future actions that can be easily guessed or told before they happen

_____ 19. the period of time when a man and woman are deciding if they will get married.

_____ 20. using old customs

A. courtship

B. equal rights

C. have their roots

D. predictable

G. generation

H. fragile

I. damsel in distress

J. traditional

F. chivalry

**Write a word in each sentence to make it correct. Choose from this list:
agree, different, fragile, rights, "ladies first."**

21. Different generations have _____ standards and values about manners between men and women.

22. In days of chivalry, men and women thought that women were _____.

23. The principle of _____ first was taught to little boys at an early age.

24. Women began to ask for equal _____ instead of chivalry.

25. Americans don't _____ about chivalry and manners between men and women.

14.　Visiting Someone in the Hospital

Do you have a friend in the hospital? Should you visit?

A person who is in the hospital for a long time may enjoy the visit of friends and family. However, if he or she is feeling very ill, a visit may *not* be welcome.

Find out from the person's family if it is OK for you to visit.

Do not visit someone if you have a cold or other illness yourself.

American hospitals have rules about visits. They have to have **security*** for patients. They need to keep the patients safe from further illness.

There may be **visiting hours*** when it is OK to visit **patients***. These times will be different in different parts of the hospital. Don't visit a patient during other times.

Usually only two visitors at a time may visit someone in a **semiprivate*** room.

Some hospitals do not allow children to visit. Find out what the rules are about children.

When you enter the hospital at the main entrance, stop at the information desk. Ask for a **visitor's pass***. Ask for directions to the patient's room. Later, you may have to show the pass to **security guards***.

When you have ended your visit, be sure to bring the pass back to the desk. This allows other visitors to go to visit the patient.

Keep the visit short. Do not tire out the patient. The patient may enjoy your visit, but needs to rest.

Do not sit on the patient's bed.

You may bring something such as a small vase of flowers, a paperback book, a magazine, a small notepad and pen, or fruit or snacks. Many hospitals have a gift store run by volunteers. Usually a patient does not have a lot of room to put things, so small gifts are best. There can also be a problem of stealing. Do not leave anything valuable with the patient.

Word Help

security *noun.* Protection against harm or theft of belongings.
visiting hours *noun, plural.* The time when hospitals allow people to visit patients.
patient *noun.* A person who goes to a doctor because of an illness or injury.
semiprivate *adjective.* Shared by two patients.
visitor's pass *noun.* A paper that gives a person permission to be in a hospital to visit a patient.

security guard *noun.* A person who keeps the hospital safe.

This is the wrong way to visit a person in the hospital.
How many bad manners can you find in this picture?

The patient may be on a special **diet***. Check with the hospital first before bringing a food gift for the patient. Do not bring **junk foods*** or alcoholic beverages to a patient. They will not help the patient get well. It is very dangerous to mix alcohol with certain medicines.

What is good conversation for a hospital visit? Listen to the patient's stories of his or her **experience*** in the hospital. Do *not* tell stories of other illnesses or of your own problems. Do not bring bad news. Talk about pleasant things. Even if the patient is seriously ill, they need to hear positive thoughts: "Modern medicine does **miracles***." "It's amazing what doctors can do these days."

Are you visiting during **meal*** time? Then bring a **snack*** for yourself while the patient eats the hospital meal. Or go to the hospital cafeteria to eat. Do not eat the patient's dinner, please.

If the patient receives a telephone call, take a short walk so he or she can talk **privately*** with the caller. Be **courteous*** to other patients in the room. Use the bathroom provided for visitors, not the patient's bathroom.

Word Help

diet *noun*. Foods that a person may eat.
junk food *noun, slang*. Food with a lot of sugar, fat, or salt in it. Food that has no value for the body.
experience *noun*. What a person knows because of their actions or because of things that have happened to them.

miracle *noun*. Wonderful things that are hard to believe; things done as if by God.
meal *noun*. breakfast, lunch, or dinner.
snack *noun*. A small amount of food.
privately *adverb*. Alone; when no one else can see or hear you.

Let's talk about it.

1. Before you visit someone in the hospital, what should you do?

2. When should you *not* visit someone in the hospital?

3. What are some hospital rules for security of the patients?

4. What are some rules for the comfort and health of the patients?

5. What are some things you might bring to a person in the hospital?

6. What topics should you avoid in a conversation with a person in the hospital?

7. Have you ever been in an American hospital? Tell about it.

8. Were you ever in a hospital in your native country? Tell about it.

Using new words:
Match the word with its meaning.

_____ 9. respectful; polite

_____ 10. a private police officer

_____ 11. time when visitors are allowed in the hospital

_____ 12. a list of things that a person may or should eat

_____ 13. things a person does, or learns, or that happen to him or her

_____ 14. alone; without others around

_____ 15. for two people (a room, for example)

_____ 16. a person who consults a doctor or goes to the hospital

_____ 17. a paper that shows that you are allowed to be in a building, such as a hospital, school, business, etc.

A. visitor's pass

B. privately

C. courteous

D. visiting hours

E. experience

F. security guard

G. patient

H. semi-private

I. diet

Write a word in each sentencve to make it correct. Choose from this list: volunteers, cold, positive, visitor's pass, illness, pleasant.

18. Do not visit someone in the hospital if you have a _____ or _____ yourself.

19. When you go to visit a friend in a hospital, stop first at the Information Desk to get a _____.

20. Many hospitals have a gift shop run by _____.

21. Talk about _____ things, not bad news or your own problems.

22. When a patient is seriously ill, he or she needs to hear _____ thoughts.

What is *clean* to Americans?

What is good **hygiene***?

U.S. **"middle-class"*** culture has certain rules about hygiene. Some of these rules are about good health. These rules are taught in school health classes.

Other rules for good hygiene are taught by parents.

Some ideas are taught by TV **commercials***.

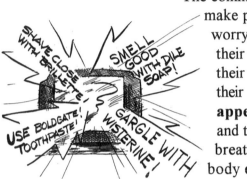

The commercials make people worry about their homes, their clothes, their **appearance***, and their hair, breath, and body **odors*** (B.O.). This helps the business sell more hygiene and cleaning products.

All in all, Americans are crazy about clean! Middle-class Americans bathe or shower at least once a day, and sometimes **twice***. They wash their hair **frequently***. They may change their clothes daily.

Word Help

hygiene *noun.* Personal cleanliness in order to stay healthy.
middle-class *noun.* The large group of people in society who value education, hard work, cleanliness, and a certain standard of manners.
commercial *noun.* Advertisement.
appearance *noun.* A person's looks: face, clothes, hair, makeup, hands, etc.
odor *noun.* A smell.
twice *adverb.* Two times.
frequently *adverb.* Often; many times during a period of time.

Rule #1: Smell good. Don't smell bad. For adults, that can mean taking a shower or bath every day. It *doesn't* mean using a *lot* of perfume or **after-shave lotion***. Other people should not notice a person's perfume from more than 2 feet away.

Most American adults who work in business offices, schools, and hospitals use an **antiperspirant*** or underarm **deodorant***. (Today, some scientists think that antiperspirants may lead to breast cancer. So it may be better to use a deodorant.)

Rule # 2: Have clean hair.

Rule # 3, for men: A man should shave daily, or keep his beard neat. He should **trim*** hair in his nose and ears, too.

Rule # 4: A woman's makeup should be **moderate***, not overly bright or thick. It's OK to wear *no* makeup at all.

Rule #5. Clean hands. The law requires food handlers to wash their hands after they use the bathroom. Parents teach their children to do the same. Washing hands is a good way to **prevent*** the spread of colds. Clean your fingernails, too.

Some newcomers say that Americans "smell funny." This may be from the large amount of

after-shave lotion *noun.* A liquid that men put on their faces after they shave. The lotion has a pleasant smell.
antiperspirant *noun.* A product that people put in their armpits to stop perspiration.
deodorant *noun.* A product that people put in their armpits to prevent a bad odor from perspiration.
trim *verb.* To cut with a small pair of scissors.
moderate *adjective.* Not overdone; using a small amount.
prevent *verb.* To stop something from happening.

meat and milk we eat. On the other hand, Americans find that some newcomers "smell funny." This can be from eating a lot of **garlic***, onions, or strong **spices***.

People usually cannot smell their own odors. Adults are too polite to **mention*** another person's odor. They just stay away.

If a child at school "smells funny," other children can be **cruel***. They may make fun of him or her. Teachers may ask the school nurse to help the child learn how to handle the problem.

School nurses may offer advice, such as:

- Take a bath or shower every day.
- Change your underwear and socks every day.
- Wash your clothes before they have a bad odor.
- Brush your teeth twice a day and after meals.
- See a dentist twice a year. Have him or her take care of any **cavities*** you may have.
- Don't eat garlic or onions for breakfast!

How clean can a floor be?

"Cleanliness is next to Godliness," is an old saying. "Her home is so clean, you can eat off the floor!" This used to be a compliment for a "good housewife." Perhaps she swept and scrubbed her kitchen floor every day.

Word Help

garlic *noun*. A strong-smelling plant used in cooking.
spices *noun*. Pepper, herbs, onions, etc. that are added to food to give it extra flavor.
mention *verb*. To say something about.
cruel acting in a way that makes someone else feel bad
cavity *noun*. A hole in a tooth.

That has changed with today's career women and working wives. "Who wants to eat off the floor?" they ask. "We have tables to eat off of." They have "better things to do" than to keep their homes as clean as their grandmothers did.

The standards for floor cleanliness are different in different cultures. Many Asians are shocked that Americans wear shoes in their homes. It seems dirty and bad-mannered to them. They always take their shoes off inside a home.

In our history, Most American homes had dirt floors. People did not sit on the floor to eat and they did not sleep on the floor. They sat on chairs, ate at tables, and slept on beds.

Americans didn't, and still don't, think of floors as "clean places". So in most homes, people can keep their shoes on when they walk into a home. (Wipe your shoes at the door, though if they are wet or muddy!) If a person has a new, light-colored carpet, he or she may ask guests to take off their shoes.

In places where people traditionally *sat* on the floor, *ate* on the floor, and *slept* on the floor, there is a different way to think about the floor. The floor *had* to be a clean place. In those cultures people always had to take off their shoes before going inside a home. They may also have had floors made of **delicate*** mats. Shoes would quickly make holes in that kind of floor.

delicate *adjective*. Easily torn or broken.

Let's talk about it.

1. What are some rules of American hygiene?

2. What are rules of hygiene in your native culture?

3. How does TV influence people's hygiene? Tell about a TV commercial for hygiene that you have seen.

4. What surprised you about American hygiene?

5. Who wears perfume in your native country—men or women, or both? Or neither? What is your opinion of perfume?

6. How is women's makeup different in the U.S. from that in your native country?

7. What are the customs about wearing shoes in the home in the U.S.? What are the customs in your native country?

8. How do you feel about wearing shoes in a house?

Using new words:
Match the word with its meaning.

_____ 9. A hole in one's tooth

_____ 10. very unkind or hurtful

_____ 11. something to put on a man's face after he shaves

_____ 12. a chemical that stops a person from perspiring under the arms

_____ 13. not too much

_____ 14. a small plant, like an onion, that has a very strong smell

_____ 15. the way a person looks to others

_____ 16. personal cleanliness

A. hygiene

B. moderate

C. garlic

D. after-shave lotion

E. antiperspirant

F. cavities

G. appearance

H. cruel

Write a word in the sentence that makes it correct. Choose from this list: twice, shoes, hygiene, bathroom, moderate.

17. Ideas about _____ are taught by parents, by schools, and by TV commercials.

18. Perfume and makeup should be _____.

19. Parents teach children to wash their hands after they use the _____.

20. Dentists tell Americans to brush their teeth _____ a day, and after eating.

21. Americans usually wear their _____ in the house.

22. That's because in their history, Americans traditionally sat on _____, and ate at tables, not on the _____.

16.   Giving a Gift, Getting a Gift

Many people give gifts to family and friends on these special **occasions***:

A birthday, wedding, **anniversary***, birth of a baby, Christmas, **retirement***, new home, high-school or college graduation, **bar mitzvah*** and **bat mitzvah***, **confirmation***, Hanukkah, Mother's Day, Father's Day, and Valentine's Day. It's a long list.

A person may give a gift to someone who has done a favor. A guest to a dinner party may bring a small gift to the **host** or **hostess***. Friends of a sick person might send a book, flowers, or a basket of fruit. Students or parents may give small presents to teachers at Christmas, or at the end of the term.

The most common gifts for nonfamily members are flowers, plants, candy, and **fancy foods***. Wine is a common hostess gift. Liquor is a common business gift.

Other gifts for people you don't know well are: **assorted*** teas, a box or tin of cookies, a basket of fruit, a **knickknack***, a candle, or a picture frame. Something from your native culture is appreciated.

A gift for a friend can be more personal when you know their likes and dislikes: clothing, music, a book, a video, or a game. Gloves, scarves, ties, belts, or jewelry all are popular gifts.

Sometimes a group of friends collect money to buy a larger gift. Many stores sell gift **certificates***. Then, the person who gets the certificate can buy what he or she wants at that store.

A person with a small income is not able to buy an expensive gift. It is not expected from him or her. People say *"It's the thought that counts."* Homemade things or home-baked foods, and even poems are appreciated. They are a special gift of your time.

At some birthday parties, or bridal showers, or baby showers, everyone watches the opening of the gifts. The guests enjoy seeing what gifts are given.

Sometimes the gift is opened **in private***.

Sometimes Americans **present*** a gift

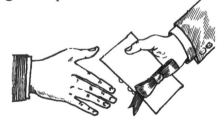

Word Help

occasion *noun*. Event; time.
anniversary *noun*. The day that celebrates something that happened in the past. "Our wedding anniversary is June 20."
retirement *noun*. The time when a person stops working, after working for many years
bar mitzvah, bat mitzvah *noun*. Religious ceremonies for Jewish children when they become 13 years old. A *bar mitzvah* is for a boy. A *bat mitzvah* is for a girl.
confirmation *noun*. A religious ceremony that marks the "strengthening" of a person's religion.
hostess *noun*. The woman who cooks a meal for guests in her house. A man is called a *host*.
fancy foods *noun, plural*. Jars or boxes of very well prepared or unusual food.

assorted *adjective*. Having many different kinds.
knickknack [nik nak] *noun*. A small object or doll that might be displayed on a shelf or desk.
certificate *noun*. A piece of paper that has a printed value on it.
in private *adverb*. Alone, without others nearby.

with two hands, but not always. Either hand may be used to give or get a gift. We may say something like *"Here's a little something for your birthday,"* or *"I got this for you; I hope you like it."* *"Put this under your Christmas tree."*

When you get a gift, you can open the gift **immediately***, or you can open it later. Ask, *"May I open it now?"* (The giver may think it's rude if you *don't* open it.)

The gift-giver may say *"Yes, open it now."* Or *"Please open it later."*

If there is a card with the gift, open the card first. Read the greeting in the card. When you open a gift, take time to **admire*** the gift, and thank the giver. Make some **comment*** about the gift and the giver: *"Thank you, it's great!" "This will look nice [on our shelf by the window]." "I have wanted one of these for a long time. How did you know?" "It's just what I need! You are so thoughtful!" "You didn't have to get me anything. This is so* **sweet*** *of you."*

Money is a common gift for children's college savings. It's also a welcome wedding gift. The amount of the gift depends on how close the giver is to the person, and the **financial condition*** of the giver. Don't give money for other occasions, however.

For a **bridal shower***, the gift is something for the couple's new home. Some couples go to a large department store and **register*** their "wish list." This is a list of many items at different prices. When you shop at the store you can ask to see the list. You can choose something that **fits your budget***. This is so the couple will not get **duplicate*** presents, or things they can't use. A wedding gift is often **cash***.

Many gifts for the home are sold in sets of four—four napkins, four place mats, four dessert dishes, etc. That is because the **typical*** family has four members. Or, a married couple may entertain one other couple.

Be sure to thank people for gifts that you did not open in front of them. Busy people may call by telephone or send a thank-you card. It is polite to write a few sentences of your own, in addition to the words on a printed card. For larger gifts, write a thank-you note even if you thanked the person at the time you received the gift. Also, **mention*** the gift again, later.

Dear Hannah,

Thank you so much for the box of chocolates. They were delicious. We saved them as a special treat at our family dinner party. It was a very thoughtful and useful gift.

Happy holidays.

Sincerely,
Madelyn

Word Help

present [pree zent'] *verb*. Give.
immediately *adverb*. Without waiting.
admire *verb*. To look at something and say nice things about it.
comment *noun*. A spoken opinion about something.
sweet *adjective*. Thoughtful; nice; kind.
financial condition *noun*. The amount of money a person earns and has in the bank, minus his or her expenses and debts to others.

bridal shower *noun*. A party given for a woman who is going to get married.
register *verb*. To go to a store and make a list of gifts that you would like.
fit your budget *verb phrase*. To be at a price that you can afford.
duplicate *adjective*. Two of the same things.
cash *noun*. Money.
typical *adjective*. Usual, average.
mention *verb*. To speak about during a conversation.

Let's talk about it.

1. What are some occasions when Americans might give a gift? What are occasions in your native country?

2. What are some common gifts to give to nonfamily members or people who are not close friends?

3. What is a gift certificate?

4. If you have no money, what are some gifts you can give?

5. What are some things you might say when you give a birthday gift?

6. In your native country, is it the custom to open gifts when you receive them, or later? Tell about it.

7. What are some things you can say when you thank a person for a gift?

8. What was the best gift you have received? Who gave it to you? How did you thank the person?

9. What is the gift you enjoyed giving the most? To whom did you give the gift? Why?

Using new words:

Match the word with its meaning.

_____ 10. A day that celebrates an event in the past, such as a wedding day

A. present

_____ 11. a gift

B. immediately

_____ 12. right now; without waiting

C. admire

_____ 13. to show that one thinks something is good, useful, or beautiful

D. anniversary

E. retirement

_____ 14. the beginning of a new life after a lifetime of work

F. assorted

_____ 15. having several different kinds of something

Write a word in each sentence to make it correct. Choose from this list: home, thank you, gift, candy, occasions, flowers, admire, thought.

16. Many people give gifts to family and friends on special
_____.

17. A guest to a dinner party may bring a small _____ to the host or hostess.

18. Common gifts for nonfamily members are
_____

19. People say, "It's not the gift; it's the _____ that counts."

20. When you open a gift, take time to _____it and thank the giver.

21. At a bridal shower, a gift is usually something for the couple's
_____.

22. You can send a _____ card to thank someone for the gift. Be sure to write a few sentences of your own.

17. What Is Sexual Harassment?

Sexual harassment* is in the news a lot. It is a new **concept*** in American manners and laws.

Sexual harassment is *repeated* behavior of a sexual nature that is *unwanted and unwelcome*.

Sexual harassment can take place at school or at one's workplace. It can occur at any other place that one cannot easily walk away from.

These are some behaviors at work or school that can be called sexual harassment:

- pressure to trade sexual favors for some reward (job, promotion, grade, etc.)

- making comments about a person's body

- unwelcome touching or closeness

- talking about one's sexual abilities

- hanging up pictures or calendars showing **nude*** women or men

- using **vulgar*** language

- telling "dirty" jokes

Unwanted sexual attention can be **offensive*** to both women and men. It can create a bad work or school environment.

Supervisors* at work are not allowed to sexually harass anyone who works for them. That's because supervisors have a lot of power over **employees***—they can **fire*** them or **transfer*** them to a different job. They control pay raises, **promotions***, and some of the **benefits*** of a job. In the past, employees who were afraid of losing their jobs **tolerated*** this **rude*** behavior, and kept quiet about it.

Most schools and colleges have rules that teachers may not date students. College professors and high-school teachers have power over their students. They give out grades, and can pass or fail a student. A professor who invites a student for a date can be accused of sexual harassment.

Word Help

sexual harassment *[huh rass' mint] noun phrase*. Repeated and unwanted actions or words of a sexual nature that bother, embarrass, insult, or upset another person.
concept *noun*. Idea.
nude *adjective*. Without clothes
vulgar *adjective*. Having to do with sex, spoken in "dirty" language.
offensive *adjective*. Insulting; unpleasant.

supervisor *noun*. A person who makes rules for, and is responsible for, a group of workers.
employee *noun*. A person who works for another person or organization.
fire *verb*. To tell a person to leave a job.
transfer *verb*. To move from one job or class to another.
promotion *noun*. An advancement to a job with more responsibility and better pay.
benefit *noun*. Something extra, such as health insurance or more vacation time.
tolerate *verb*. To accept without complaining.
rude *adjective*. Bad-mannered; impolite.

Groups of people might enjoy telling dirty jokes at work. Or they often make sexual **comments***. In the past, a person who was **offended*** had to be quiet about it. The offended person could not easily ask the others to stop the behavior.

There now are laws against sexual harassment. Schools must protect their students from harassment. Business companies must protect their employees from harassment. Both men and women must be careful of their words and deeds in regard to sexual matters.

If an employer, teacher, **coworker***, or classmate does something that is sexually offensive to you, ask the person to stop. If the behavior does not stop, (or you are afraid to ask), you should report the behavior to *that*

person's supervisor. The supervisor should have a meeting with the person to explain the behavior that is causing a problem.

It's a good idea, too, to dress **modestly*** to school and work. It is not **appropriate*** to wear mini skirts, low cut blouses, open shirts, falling pants, tight pants, and other sexually suggestive clothing.

What about people at a job who like each other? Can't a person ask another person out for a date? Can't coworkers fall in love?

Of course they can. Sexual harassment is *unwanted* behavior.

However, the workplace is considered a dangerous place to look for love! Most **romances*** end after a while. If someone is hurt, there can be bad feelings at the workplace.

(Adapted from **Dangerous English 2000!** *by Elizabeth Claire.* Delta Systems*).*

Word Help

comment *noun*. A spoken opinion.
offend *verb*. To hurt another's feelings, or make a person angry by one's words or actions.
members of the opposite sex *noun phrase*. People who are not the same sex you are. If you are a male, then girls and women are members of the opposite sex.

coworker [co′ wur′ ker] *noun*. A person who works in the same place.
modestly *adverb*. In a manner that does not call attention to one's sex.
bellybutton *noun*. The umbilicus; the mark left on a person's abdomen since birth.
romance* *noun*. The beginning stage of a love relationship.

Let's talk about it.

1. What are some behaviors that could be called sexual harassment?

2. Are these behaviors OK in your native country?

3. What's your opinion about these behaviors?

4. What can you do if you feel someone at school or at work is sexually harassing you?

Using new words:
Match the word with its meaning.

_____ 5. an idea

_____ 6. hurt someone's feelings or values

_____ 7. to end an employee's job

_____ 8. rude, impolite, "lower-class" language

_____ 9. a change to a better job with the same employer

_____ 10. repeated behavior (such as touching or making comments about a person's body) that is not wanted

_____ 11. without clothing

_____ 12. to accept willingly; to allow without objecting

A. sexual harassment

B. offend

C. concept

D. nude

E. vulgar

F. tolerate

G. fire

H. promotion

Write a word in each sentence to make it correct. Choose from this list: stop, unwanted, protect, walk away, offended, supervisor.

13. Sexual harassment is behavior that is _____ from a member of the opposite sex.

14. Sexual harassment can take place at any place a person cannot easily _____ from.

15. In the past, a person who was _____ by unwanted sexual behavior was quiet about it. It was considered "natural behavior."

16. Schools and business companies must _____ their students or employees from sexual harassment.

17. If a coworker says something that is sexually offensive to you, ask the person to _____. If you are afraid to ask, report the behavior to their _____.

18.

Showing Emotions

In general, Americans show *more* of their emotions and feelings than Asians do. Americans show *less* of their feelings than South Americans or people from southern European countries or the Middle East.

Of course, there are many **exceptions***. Americans come from many different **ethnic backgrounds***. They have different kinds of education and family experience. They have different feelings about the same event.

For these reasons, Americans cannot use **intuition*** about other people's feelings. Americans understand each other better when they openly express their feelings.

Many Americans solve problems with a **direct approach***.

Assertive*, **self-confident*** people say directly how they feel, what they like or don't like, and what they want. They expect others to do the same.

Americans who cannot assert themselves might feel that other people "**walk all over them***." There are classes in "assertiveness training" to help people speak up for themselves. On the other hand, Americans don't like people who seem "too

pushy*." It's good to be assertive without being selfish. **Consider*** the other person's needs as you express yourself and ask for what you want.

Tact* is the ability to say things without hurting another person's feelings. Americans admire a tactful person. However, tact is not very common! Using a direct approach can often hurt another's feelings without intending to.

Some people are very "**touchy*.**" They are easily hurt by unkind words or a thoughtless **comment***. A person might **avoid*** a neighbor, friend, or even a family member because of something the other person said years ago.

Often, Americans don't *say* exactly how they are feeling, but they *show* it on their faces or by their body **posture***.

Families teach their children about showing or hiding emotions. In the past, it was common for parents to tell little boys they mustn't cry. On the other hand, girls were allowed to show their feelings. Grown men may feel uncomfortable with showing their sad feelings or pain.

Word Help

exception *noun.* Something that doesn't fit in with the rules just given, or the standard.
ethnic background *noun.* A person's national heritage, language, and customs.
intuition *noun.* An inner wisdom that gives us a feeling about a person.
direct approach *noun phrase.* Clear, and easy to understand communication, without expecting another person to guess one's meaning.
assertive *adjective.* Able to ask for what one wants, and to express one's opinions.
self-confident *adjective.* Sure of one's worth.
walk all over someone *idiom.* To take what one needs and wants without thinking about the needs or wishes of the other person.

pushy *adjective.* Aggressive; asking for things and taking things in a rude way, without thinking about others' needs; telling others what to do, without using polite manners.
consider *verb.* To think about.
tact *noun.* The ability to tell the truth without hurting a person's feelings.
touchy *adjective.* Easily upset by what someone says or does.
comment *noun.* A spoken opinion.
avoid *verb.* To stay away from someone or something.
posture *noun.* The way a person stands or sits.

70

Today's parents tell their children to **express*** their emotions.

In general, Americans will let the people around them know if they are feeling happy, sad, angry, upset, **bored***, sleepy, worried, or surprised. We show our excitement and interest. We don't worry too much that our bad feelings will make another person feel sad. In fact, sometimes we like **sympathy***.

Americans are uncomfortable with too much politeness and with too many **compliments***. Americans will tell **"little white lies*"** in order not to hurt someone's feelings. But, in general, we like people who are **sincere***. We don't like **"phony***" people.

People who are "in love" often walk down the street holding hands. They may hug and touch each other. Young people are not embarrassed to kiss their sweetheart in public. (Older people may be embarrassed to see it, however.)

These public **displays*** of **affection*** are surprising to newcomers. Many Americans would say this is bad manners. But some young people are not **inhibited*** by older people's opinions.

Word Help

express *verb*. To say or show what one is feeling.
bored *adjective*. Tired because there is nothing interesting to do.
sympathy *noun*. A showing of compassion for another person's problems or pain.
compliment *noun*. A nice comment about a person. "Good work!" "Your baby is cute," are compliments.
little white lie *noun*. A "small" lie that a person tells in order not to hurt another person's feelings.
sincere *adjective*. Honest; telling one's true feelings.
phony *adjective*. Not real; pretending to like someone that you don't really like; not sincere.

display *noun*. A show of something so that others may see it.
affection *noun*. Hugs, kisses, touching, etc. between people who love each other.
inhibited. *adjective*. Caused to be less expressive or less able to show one's emotions.

Let's talk about it.

1. Does your native culture encourage full expression of all feelings?

2. Do Americans seem different in expressing their feelings? Tell about it.

3. Which of these feelings are easy for you to express: *anger, sadness, joy, embarrassment, boredom, excitement, appreciation, sleepiness, worry, surprise, upset.* Which ones are *difficult* to express?

4. What is the direct approach?

5. Are you assertive? Are assertive people admired in your native country?

6. What can be done if "people walk all over you"?

7. What is tact? Give an example.

8. Do you know any "touchy" people?

9. What are some "little white lies" that people might tell?

10. Is it OK for couples to hold hands or kiss in public in your native country? What's your opinion about it?

Using new words:
Match the word with its meaning.

_____ 11. the way a person stands or sits

_____ 12. able to tell others directly what they want or think

_____ 13. easily hurt or upset by other people's words or actions

_____ 14 take from a person without giving anything in return; dominate

_____ 15. a feeling about something that you can't explain

_____ 16. something that doesn't follow the rules, or is not included in a group

_____ 17. an ability to tell the truth without hurting someone's feelings

_____ 18. honest, in a kind, thoughtful way.

_____ 19. not honest; pretending to be friendly and kind

A. phony

B. exception

C. assertive

D. touchy

E. sincere

F. tact

G. walk all over a person

H. posture

I. intuition

Write a word in each sentence to make it correct. Choose from this list: cry, sincere, affection, express, intuition, assertive, admire, phony.

20. _____ people say directly what they think; they tell what they like and don't like, and they ask for what they want.

21. Americans _____ a tactful person.

22. In the past, it was common for parents to tell their children that "little boys don't _____."

23. Today's parents encourage children to _____ their emotions.

24. Americans like people who are _____. They don't like _____ people.

25. Public showing of _____ by boyfriend and girlfriend is surprising to newcomers. It is offensive to some older people.

19. Telephone Manners

The telephone companies used to tell people that it is helpful and polite to answer the telephone with more than just a "hello."

They suggested things like

"Hello, this is Jack."

"Hello, this is the Smith residence."

But most Americans feel that is too **formal***. Some people feel it is not safe to give unknown callers any information. So almost everyone just says *"Hello."*

A simple conversation goes like this:

"Hello."

"Hello. This is Nancy Metz. Can I talk to Jack Smith?"

"Just a minute." Or, *"Jack can't come to the phone right now. Can I take a **message***?"*

(If you don't know who you are talking to, it is not wise to tell them that a husband or parent isn't home.)

"Please tell him to call me."

"OK. Can I have your telephone number?"

"Yes, it's 201-555-1111."

"201-555-1111?"

"That's right."

"How do you spell your last name?"

"Metz: M-E-T-Z."

"OK, Nancy, I'll tell him you called."

"Thanks. Good bye."

People often get calls from **telemarketers***. Telemarketers may be selling doctor services, telephone service, vacation trips, or credit cards. Some telemarketers call to ask for **donations*** to **charities***.

"Hello, may I speak to Jack Smith?"

"This is Jack Smith speaking."

*"Jack, I'm calling you **on behalf of*** the Poor People of America."*

"Thank you, I'm not interested."

Or, you can say:

I'm sorry, I don't speak English well. Good-bye.

Politely tell the caller you are not interested, then hang up the telephone.

There are many telephone **scams***. *Never* give your credit card number to *anyone* who calls you. The person may not be calling for the group he says he represents.

If someone calls you and says, *"Congratulations! You have won a free vacation at the Blahblah*

Word Help

formal *adjective*. Official, importan- sounding; following set rules for behavior.
message *noun*. Information that a person tells another person.

telemarketer *noun*. A salesperson who uses the telephone to find customers.
donation *noun*. A gift.
charity *noun*. An organization that collects money for people who need help.
on behalf of *prepositional phrase*. For; representing a group of people.
scam *noun*. A plan to get money by tricking a person with lies.

Hotel!" don't get excited! It will cost you money. You will have to pay the air fare to get to the free hotel. Just say *"No, thank you,"* and hang up.

Do you get too many calls from telemarketers? You can register your telephone number with the national **"Do Not Call List*."** Most calls will stop after a few months.

At work, good telephone manners are very important. Your voice and your manners help your company stay in business! Ask your employer how to answer the phone. Each company has a different way. Some examples may be: *"Easy English NEWS, this is Tina."* Or, *"This is Morely's Supermarket, Tom Black speaking. How may I help you?"*

If the call is for someone else, you may have conversations like:

"I'd like to speak with Sally Green."

"I'm sorry, Sally is away from her desk at the moment. May I take your name and number and have her call you back?"

Or, *"I'm sorry, Sally is in a meeting. May I take a message?"*

Always be sure to get a telephone number. Write the message down and give it to the person it's for.

If you can't talk on the telephone at the moment, you can say, *"I'd love to talk to you, but I was just [going out the door]. What's a good time to call you back?*

Cell phones are very useful. Good cell-phone manners will help the people around you.

Don't take a call when you are in a meeting, church, theater, class, bus, or any place where a call will **disturb*** other people. Turn your ringer off!

When you talk on a cell phone, move away from other people (10 to 15 feet) so your conversation can be private, and not disturb others. Speak in a normal tone. We don't want to hear other people's conversation, we are thinking our own quiet thoughts.

Talking on a cell phone **distracts*** a person. This can be very dangerous. Don't talk on the phone when you are crossing streets, using machinery, or driving a car. Many states have laws now to prevent accidents by "distracted drivers."

Word Help

Do not call list. A government list that telemarketers must use to make sure they are not calling people who do not want to be called. You can register your telephone number on this list at the website "www.Donotcall.com"

disturb *verb*. To annoy or bother a person.
distract *verb*. To make a person lose awareness of what he or she is doing.

Let's talk about it.

1. What's a good way to answer the telephone?

2. How do you answer the telephone at your house?

3. Do you answer the telephone at your job? How do you answer?

4. How do businesses answer the telephone in your native country?

5. Have you had problems using the telephone in the U.S.? Tell about it.

6. Have you had calls from telemarketers? Tell about it.

7. What can you do when a telemarketer calls?

8. Should you give personal information to strangers on the telephone? Tell three reasons why not.

9. What are some cell-phone manners?

10. What are some cell-phone dangers?

76

Using new words:
Match the word with its meaning.

_____ 11. information that a person tells another person

_____ 12. a salesperson who uses the telephone to find customers

_____ 13. an organization that collects money for people who need help

_____ 14. a plan to steal money from people by telling lies

_____ 15. to annoy or bother a person

_____ 16. to make a person lose awareness of what he or she is doing

_____ 17. for another person or group

_____ 18. to cut off the telephone connection

A. disturb

B. distract

C. message

D. telemarketer

E. on behalf of

F. charity

G. scam

H. hang up

Write a word in each sentence to make it correct. Choose from this list: message, spell, private, cell phone, polite, register, bother.

19. It is helpful and _____ to answer the telephone with more than just a "hello."

20. Jack isn't home right now. Can I take a _____?

21. How do you _____ your last name?

22. If you get too many calls from telemarketers, you can _____ your phone number with a national "Do not call list."

23. Don't let your cell phone ring in places where it will _____ other people.

24. When you talk on a cell phone, move away from other people so your conversation can be _____.

25. Don't talk on a _____ when you are driving a car or crossing a street.

20. Road Manners

There are many laws about driving.

We must drive on the right side of the road.

We must **obey*** the speed limit.

We must not go the wrong way on a one-way street.

We may not drive on the sidewalk.

When you are driving on the highway, there are rules that tell which car must **yield*** to other cars. We say that the **vehicle*** that may go first has the "**right-of-way***."

For example, a car that is going straight has the right-of-way over a car that is waiting on a side road to enter the **flow of traffic***.

There are also ways to show **courtesy*** on the highway. Courtesy on the road helps other drivers have a good experience. It helps improve safety, too.

In some cases, drivers may give other drivers the right-of-way. This courtesy keeps traffic flowing. It prevents many accidents.

There are traffic rules for **pedestrians*** on the streets. Pedestrians have the right-of-way at **crosswalks***. Nevertheless, they should still look both ways before crossing.

Of course, cars must stop even if a pedestrian is **jaywalking***. In some cities, **jaywalkers*** can get a ticket. It's good driving manners to politely wait for people to cross the street.

Bicycles have to follow traffic laws, too. In cities, bicycles may not go on the sidewalk. They must go in the street. There may be special bike **lanes*** for bicycles in some places.

It is dangerous for children to ride a bicycle in the streets. Children may ride in parks or in special areas. Children must wear **helmets*** when riding. It's a good idea for *any* rider to wear a helmet. A helmet

Word Help

obey *verb*. Follow a law or an order from someone.
yield *verb*. To slow or stop in order to give another person or car the right to go first.
vehicle [vee′ uh kuhl] *noun*. A car, bus, motorcycle, truck, etc.
right-of-way *noun*. The legal right to pass first, while other cars must slow or stop.
flow of traffic *noun*. The movement of cars and other vehicles on a road.

courtesy *noun*. Good manners; politeness.
pedestrian [puh des′ tree uhn] *noun*. A person who is walking.
crosswalk *noun*. A place that is marked with painted white lines to show where people should walk across the street.
jaywalk *verb*. To walk across a street in an illegal way such as against a red light, or in the middle of a block.
jaywalker *noun*. A person who jaywalks.
lane *noun*. A part of the street that is marked with lines for cars or bicycles. "Drivers should stay in their lane except to pass another car."
helmet *noun*. A hard hat that protects a person's head.

78

can save your life. Bike riders should know that pedestrians have the right of way over bicycles.

All drivers must try to avoid accidents, even if they have the right-of-way.

Road rage*

Near large cities, there are **traffic jams*** every day during **rush hour***. Drivers have to wait for a long time to stop for red lights and pay tolls on bridges. Construction on the road can slow the traffic down, too. So can an accident, or someone changing a flat tire.

Some people may get upset when they are late. They may get upset when someone **cuts them off*** after passing them in their car. Drivers may get upset if another driver makes a mistake that causes a dangerous situation.

A few drivers become **rude***. They honk their horns loudly. They may **insult*** other drivers. They may drive dangerously. They may stop, get out of their car, and want to fight. This rude and angry behavior is called *road rage*.

One angry driver can make other drivers angry, too. Sometimes **violence*** is the result.

The government wants drivers to **calm down.*** If someone is rude, don't get upset. It's

not personal. The other driver has a problem. Try to get away from anyone who is driving **recklessly*** or who shows anger on the road.

Good manners are especially important on the roadway. Don't honk your horn except when necessary. Don't make any rude **gestures*** at other drivers.

A moving car is a very dangerous object. If another driver does something that upsets you,

keep cool*. Don't try to do something in return. This may make the other person angrier. Get the license number of the car. Give the angry person the right-of-way. *Get out of their way.* Later, send a letter to the Department of Motor Vehicles in your state's capital city. Describe the dangerous driving, and give the license number of the car.

Word Help

rage *noun*. Extreme anger; uncontrolled fury.
traffic jam *noun*. A condition on a road when cars cannot move, or move very slowly.
rush hour *noun phrase*. When the most people are on the road going to or coming home from work.
cut a person off *idiom*. To suddenly drive a car into the lane of another car, causing a dangerous situation.
rude *adjective*. Not polite; without good manners.
insult *verb*. To say something that hurts someone's feelings.
violence *noun*. Using force to hurt another person.

calm down *verb*. To become quiet and stop being upset.
recklessly *adverb*. Without proper care; dangerously.
gesture *noun*. A movement of the hand or fingers. A rude gesture is holding up one's middle finger, or making a threatening movement as if to punch someone.
keep cool *idiom*. Stay calm; don't get upset.

Let's talk about it.

1. What are some laws about driving?

2. How are driving laws different in your native country?

3. Are there any new laws you think would be good?

4. Where should pedestrians cross the street?

5. What does it mean if a driver "gives the right of way" to another driver? When is this a good idea?

6. What is jaywalking?

7. Who has the right of way, a jaywalker or a car? Why?

8. What are some dangerous driving actions you have seen in the U.S.?

9. What causes "road rage"?

10. What can you do if another driver drives in a dangerous manner?

Using new words:
Match the word with its meaning.

_____ 11. cars, trucks, and buses moving in a street

_____ 12. extreme anger while driving a car

_____ 13. a person who is walking

_____ 14. to give the right-of-way to another car

_____ 15. a person crossing the street in the middle of the block

_____ 16. good manners

_____ 17 a space on a road for cars or bikes, marked by painted lines

_____ 18. Don't get angry or upset. (slang)

_____ 19. not carefully

_____ 20. A car, truck, bus, or motorcycle, for example

A. yield

B. road rage

C. recklessly

D. vehicle

E. Keep cool.

F. flow of traffic

G. courtesy

H. pedestrian

I. lane

J. jay walker

Write a word in the sentence that makes it correct. Choose from these words: traffic, obey, right-of-way, dangerous, recklessly.

21. Drivers must _____ the speed limit.

22. A car that is going straight ahead has the _____ over a car that is entering the flow of traffic.

23. Near big cities, there are _____ jams every day during rush hour.

24. Try to get away from anyone who is driving _____.

25. A moving car is a very _____ object.

Answers

1. Please. Thank You. (etc.)

7. C
8. D
9. G
10. H
11. A
12. B
13. F
14. E
15. end
16. appreciated
17. compliment
18. overdo

2. American Names, part I

10. C
11. F
12. E
13. D
14. B
15. A
16. G
17. H
18. Ms.
19. Ms. Joan Smith; Mrs. Joan Wilson; Mrs. David Wilson; Ms. Joan Smith Wilson
20. a. Dr.
    b. Professor
    c. Sister
    d. Rabbi
    e. Reverend
    f. Mrs.
    g. Father

3. American Names, part II

12. C
13. B
14. F
15. A
16. G
17. D
18. E
19. relative
20. father
21. names
22. girls
23. Smith
24. pronounce and remember

4. Meeting People

8. F
9. D
10. A
11. B
12. E
13. G
14. C
15. one
16. stand
17. firm
18. honesty
19. meet
20. yourself
21. repeat

5. Small Talk

17. C
18. A
19. F
20. B
21. D
22. E
23. nothing
24. health
25. sports
26. conversation

6. Smile!

6. C
7. F
8. D
9. B
10. A
11. E
12. communicate
13. language
14. welcome
15. teeth

7. Body Language

10. I
11. D
12. C
13. A
14. J
15. G
16. B
17. F
18. look
19. polite
20. arm's
21. eye contact
22. hug

8. Door Manners

9. B
10. I
11. E
12. H
13. A
14. D
15. C
16. G
17. F
18. mysterious
19. behind
20. I'm sorry.
21. nearest
22. off
23. rude

9. Coughs and Sneezes

8. C
9. D
10. A
11. B
12. F
13. E
14. blow
15. running
16. Excuse me
17. eating
18. cover
19. God bless you.
20. symptoms
21. silly

10. Table Manners, part I

16. I
17. A
18. H
19. G
20. J
21. F
22. D
23. E
24. B
25. C

11. Table Manners, part II

12. F
13. B
14. A
15. E
16. J
17. C
18. D
19. G
20. I
21. H
22. compliment
23. unpleasant
24. help
25. family

12. Restaurant Manners

11. D
12. B
13. F
14. E
15. C
16. G
17. A
18. busy
19. nonsmoking
20. rude
21. pay
22. tip

13. Manners Between Men and Women

12. H
13. C
14. B
15. I
16. G
17. F
18. D
19. A
20. J
21. different
22. fragile
23. "ladies first"
24. rights
25. agree

14. Visiting Someone in the Hospital

9. C
10. F
11. D
12. I
13. E
14. B
15. H
16. G
17. A
18. cold, illness
19. visitor's pass
20. volunteers
21. pleasant
22. positive

15. How Clean Can You Get?

9. F
10. H
11. D
12. E
13. B
14. C
15. G
16. A
17. hygiene
18. moderate
19. bathroom
20. twice
21. shoes
22. chairs, floor

16. Giving a Gift, Getting a Gift

10. D
11. A
12. B
13. C
14. E
15. F
16. occasions
17. gift
18. flowers, plants, candy, food.
19. thought
20. admire
21. home
22. thank you

17. Sexual Harassment

5. C
6. B
7. G
8. E
9. H
10. A
11. D
12. F
13. unwanted
14. walk away
15. offended
16. protect
17. stop, supervisor

18. Showing Emotions

11. H
12. C
13. D
14. G
15. I
16. B
17. F
18. E
19. A
20. assertive
21. admire
22. cry
23. express
24. sincere, phony
25. affection

19. Telephone Manners

11. C
12. D
13. F
14. G
15. A
16. B
17. E
18. H
19. polite
20. message
21. spell
22. register
23. disturb
24. private
25. cell phone

20. Road Manners

11. F
12. B
13. H
14. A
15. J
16. G
17. I
18. E
19. C
20. D
21. obey
22. right-of- way
23. traffic
24. recklessly
25. dangerous

Glossary

Some of the words in the glossary have many meanings.
We give only the meanings that you need for this book.

abbreviation [uh bree vee ay/ shin] *noun.* A short written form.
admire [ad miyr/] *verb.* To look at something and say nice things about it.
affection *noun.* Hugs, kisses, touching, etc., between people who love each other.
after-shave lotion *noun.* A liquid that men put on their faces after they shave. The lotion usually has a pleasant smell.
allow *verb.* To permit; to let someone do something.
Amen [ay/ men/ or ah/ men/] *noun.* A word used after a prayer. It means "May it be as you say."
anniversary *noun.* The day that celebrates something that happened in the past. "Our wedding anniversary is June 20."
announce *verb.* Give information or speak in a strong voice.
antiperspirant *noun.* A product that people put on the skin in their armpits to stop perspiration.
apologize *verb.* To say that you are sorry for something you did or forgot to do.
appearance *noun.* A person's looks: face, clothes, hair, makeup, hands, etc.
appetizer *noun.* A small amount of food that you eat before the main meal.
appreciate *verb.* To show or tell a person that you are thankful for their gift or favor.
arm's length *noun.* The distance from an adult's shoulder to the hand, about 30 inches.
ashes *noun.* The gray powder that is left after something is burned by fire.
assertive *adjective.* Able to ask for what one wants, and express one's opinions.
assorted *adjective.* Of many different kinds.
avoid *verb.* To stay away from someone or something; to prevent something from happening.
back away *verb phrase.* To move backward.

bar mitzvah, bat mitzvah *noun.* Religious ceremonies for Jewish children when they become 13 years old. A *bar mitzvah* is for a boy. A *bat mitzvah* is for a girl.
barrier *noun.* A wall or fence to keep a person out.
belch *noun.* A loud noise of gas coming up from the stomach and through the mouth.
benefit *noun.* Something extra, such as health insurance or more vacation time.
beverage *noun.* Something to drink: water, milk, juice, soda, beer, wine.
birth certificate *noun.* The document with information about a baby's birth: the time, place, parents' names, etc.
bless *verb.* To give God's help and protection.
blow (your nose) *verb phrase.* To close your mouth and blow mucous out of your nose and into a handkerchief or tissue.
bored *adjective.* Tired because there is nothing interesting to do.
bow one's head *verb phrase.* To look down, and have one's head turned down.
brag *verb.* To speak well of oneself, telling of one's good points, accomplishments, money, etc.
brave deeds *noun phrase.* Courageous acts; good works.
bridal shower *noun.* A party given for a woman who is going to get married.
buffet [buh fay/] **style** *adverb.* Serving oneself from plates of food all on one table. The guests line up, take a plate, and help themselves to the things they want.
bundle *noun.* A package that one is carrying.
burp *verb.* To allow air from your stomach to come up noisily through your mouth.
butt *noun.* The end of a cigarette, left when it is too short to smoke.

calm [kahm] **down** *verb.* To become quiet and stop being upset.
cancel *verb.* Stop something from happening.
cash *noun.* Money.
casserole [kas/ er ohl *noun.* A meal with rice or pasta, meat, vegetables, and sauce that is prepared in one large pot or pan and baked in the oven.
catch *verb.* To hear well. To get an illness. To understand a joke.
cavity *noun.* A hole in a tooth.
certificate *noun.* A piece of paper that has a value or important information printed.
charge *verb.* To pay a bill by credit card.
charity *noun.* An organization that collects money for people who need help.
chat *verb.* To have a pleasant conversation about topics that are not very serious.
check *noun.* A bill for the cost of dinner.
chivalry [shi/ vuhl ree] *noun.* A system of manners in which men are helpful to women and weaker people.
code of behavior *noun phrase.* A set of rules to guide a person's actions.
command *noun.* An order from a general or captain to a person of lesser power.
comment 1. *noun.* A spoken opinion. 2. *verb.* To say something about; to give an opinion on something.
commercial *noun.* Advertisement.
communicate *verb.* To speak or write one's ideas so another person can understand what you mean.
complain *verb.* To tell something bad or wrong about something.
compliment 1. *noun.* A word or words that say something nice about a person. 2. *verb.* To tell a person that you think he or she is

85

good, kind, beautiful, etc. "Good work!" and "Your baby is cute," are compliments.

concept *noun*. Idea.

confirmation *noun*. A religious ceremony that marks the "strengthening" of a person's religion.

consider *verb*. To think about.

controversial *adjective*. Having ideas that people have different opinions about; causing disagreements and arguments.

conversation *noun*. Two or more people talking and listening to each other.

courteous *adjective*. Polite; well-behaved; pleasant and respectful.

courtesy *[kehr' tuh see] noun*. Good manners; politeness.

courtship *noun*. The time when a man and women get to know each other and try to make a good impression. This is usually before marriage.

coworker *[co' wer' ker] noun*. A person who works in the same place.

crosswalk *noun*. A place that is marked with painted white lines to show where people should walk across the street.

cruel *adjective*. Hurtful; very unkind and mean.

crush *verb*. To press something very hard, in order to hurt or break it.

custom *noun*. A way of doing something that has been around for a long time.

customary *adverb*. Usual; commonly done.

cut a person off *idiom*. To suddenly drive a car into the lane of another car, causing a dangerous situation.

cutlery *[kuht' ler ee] noun*. Knives, forks, and spoons.

damsel in distress *noun phrase*. A young woman who needs someone to rescue her from danger or trouble.

date *noun*. A meeting at a set time to do something with a boyfriend or girlfriend.

delicate *adjective*. Easily torn or broken.

deodorant *[dee oh' dor unt] noun*. A product that people put on the skin iunder their arms to prevent a bad odor from perspiration.

dessert *[duh zert'] noun*. A sweet food eaten at the end of a meal: ice cream, cake, pie, fruit, etc.

diet *[diy' it] noun*. Foods that a person may eat.

dig right in *Idiom, slang*. Start eating.

digestion. *noun*. The process [in the stomach and intestines] of turning food into usuable materials for your body.

direct approach *noun phrase*. Clear, easy to understand, without expecting another person to understand what is not spoken.

disabled *[dis ay' buhld] adjective*. Not able to fully use one's arms, legs, eyes, etc.

disagree *verb*. To have a different opinion about something.

display *noun*. A show of something so that others may see it.

distant *adjective*. Having no emotional warmth; seeming not to care about another person.

distract *verb*. To take a person's attention away from what he or she is doing.

disturb *verb*. To make noises or do things that will annoy people.

do not call list. *noun phrase*. A government list that telemarketers must use to make sure they are not calling people who do not want to be called. You can register your telephone number on this list at the website "Donotcall.com"

document *noun*. Important paper.

doggy bag *noun phrase, slang*. A container you take home that contains food you were not able to finish at the restaurant. It is not for your dog; it's for *you* to eat later.

donation *noun*. A gift.

dreadfully *adverb*. An intensifier: very, very.

duplicate *[doo' pli kuht] adjective*. Two of the same thing.

elderly *adjective*. Old.

embarrassed *verb, past participle*. Ashamed or feeling foolish because of doing or saying something wrong.

employee *noun*. A person who

works for another person or organization.

entrée *noun*. The main part of a dinner.

equal rights *noun, plural*. The rights to get an education, study any subject, do any kind of work, and earn equal pay for equal work.

escort *noun*. A leader of a group that is going someplace; a man accompanying a woman to a party, restaurant, or any public place.

ethnic background *noun*. A person's national heritage, language, and customs.

etiquette *[et' ih kit] noun*. A set of rules, customs, principles, and manners for social behavior.

exception *noun*. Something that seems to be outside of a set of rules or a standard.

exist *verb*. Be; have life.

experience *noun*. What a person knows because of their actions or because of things that have happened to them.

express *verb*. To say or show what one is feeling.

eye contact *noun phrase*. The meeting of two people's eyes when they look at each other.

family name *noun*. The father's last name. His wife and children usually use it as their last name.

fancy foods *noun, plural*. Jars or packages of very delicious, tasty, or unusual food.

financial condition *noun*. The amount of money a person earns and has in the bank, minus his or her expenses and debts to others.

fire *verb*. To tell a person to leave a job.

first impression *noun phrase*. The first idea you have about a person, as soon as you meet him or her.

fit your budget *verb phrase*. To be at a price that you can afford.

flat tire *noun*. A car's tire that has lost its air.

flow of traffic *noun*. The movement of cars and other vehicles on a road.

formal *adjective*. Following fixed rules for behavior or dress; behavior at important occasions; official.

formal dinner *noun phrase*. A meal that has some fixed rules about its appearance, order of serving, and manners. People dress in good clothes, and use their "best manners."

formula *noun.* A set of steps for doing something; a set of rules to make something work.

found *verb.* To start a business or organization (past tense = founded).

fragile [fra/ jil] *adjective.* Delicate; easily hurt or broken.

frequently *adverb.* Often; many times during a period of time.

garlic *noun.* A strong-smelling plant used in cooking.

generation *noun.* A set of people who were born around the same time: "My grandmother's *generation* believed that women should not vote."

germs *noun, plural.* Bacteria that cause illness.

gesture *noun.* A movement of the hand or fingers. A rude gesture is to hold up one's middle finger.

gesundheit! [guh zunt/ hiyt] *noun.* A German word that means "Good health to you!"

given name *noun.* A name that parents choose for a child—such as John, Miguel, Anna, Jessica.

gland *noun.* One of many small organs of the body; it has the job of producing hormones, endorphins, digestive juices, etc.

go dutch *idiom.* Each person in a group pays for his or her own ticket, dinner, cost of admission, etc.

Grace *noun.* A prayer of thanks before eating.

greasy *adjective.* Oily, from the fat of meat or butter.

greet *verb.* To say hello.

grip *verb.* To hold firmly, but not tightly.

have their roots *verb phrase.* Began in some early form.

head and foot [of the table] *noun.* On a rectangular table, the two opposite short sides.

Hebrew *noun.* The people and language of the Jews.

heel *noun.* The back part of a foot.

helmet *noun.* A hard hat that protects a person's head.

hinge [hinj] *noun.* A small device that holds a door to the door

frame, and allows the door to swing.

host, hostess *noun.* The person who greets people at a restaurant; the person who invited you to dinner or a party. A hostess is female. A host can be male or female.

hygiene *[hiy/ jeen/] noun.* Personal cleanliness in order to stay healthy.

immediately *adverb.* Without waiting.

in private *adverb.* Alone, without others nearby.

include *verb.* To make someone a part of a group.

informal *adjective.* Casual, not official; ordinary, day-to-day.

inhibited. *adjective.* Caused to be less expressive or less able to show one's emotions.

initial [ih nih/ shil] *noun.* The first letter of a name.

insult *verb.* To say something that hurts someone's feelings.

interpret *verb.* To give or tell the meaning of words or actions

interrupt *verb.* To start speaking before the other person has finished speaking.

introduce *verb.* Tell people each other's names so they can know each other.

intuition [in too ish/ uhn] *noun.* An inner wisdom that gives us a feeling about a person.

invent *verb.* To make something up; to create a new thing.

invisible *adjective.* Cannot be seen.

jaywalk *verb.* To walk across a street in an illegal way, such as against a red light, or in the middle of a block.

jaywalker *noun.* A person who crosses a street in an illegal manner.

junior *adjective.* The younger one; the son of a man with the same name.

junk food *noun, slang.* Food with a lot of sugar, fat, or salt in it. Food that has very little value for the body.

keep cool *idiom.* Stay calm; don't get upset.

knickknack [nik nak] *noun.* A small object or doll that might be displayed on a shelf or desk.

knight [niyt] **in shining armor** *noun phrase.* A man (in children's fairy tales) who will take care of all the problems.

knight *noun.* In the 1300s and 1400s, a soldier of the upper class. When in battle, he wore armor and rode on horseback.

lack *verb.* To *not* have [something].

lane *noun.* A part of the street that is marked with lines for cars or bicycles. "Drivers should stay in their lane except to pass another car."

language barrier *noun phrase.* The difficulty or wall between people who speak different languages. It stops them from communicating well.

lap *noun.* The flat area formed by your upper legs, when you sit down.

lend *verb.* (past form: lent) To let another person use something that belongs to you.

limp *adjective.* Not firm; having no energy or strength.

little white lie *noun.* A "small" lie that a person tells in order not to hurt another person's feelings.

maiden name *noun.* A woman's last name before she is married.

maitre d' [mae/ truh dee/] *noun.* A person who greets people in an expensive restaurant, and leads them to a table.

make a reservation *verb phrase.* Call in advance to ask a restaurant to reserve (save) a table for you at a certain time.

make eye contact *idiom.* To look at someone who is looking at you.

meal *noun.* Breakfast, lunch, or dinner; an amount of food that will keep a person from being hungry for a few hours.

members of the opposite sex *noun phrase.* People who are not the same sex you are. If you are a male, then girls and women are members of the opposite sex.

mention [men/ shin] *verb.* To say the name of a person or subject during a conversation or a speech.

message *noun.* Information that a person tells another person.

87

metal *noun*. A hard, shiny material such as silver, gold, brass, iron, tin, copper, etc.

middle name *noun*. A name between the first name and last name. It is a second given name. It may also be a family name, such as the mother's maiden name.

middle-class *noun*. The large group of people in society who value education, hard work, cleanliness, and a certain standard of manners.

minimum *adjective*. The smallest amount.

miracle *noun*. Wonderful things that are hard to believe; things done as if by God.

misunderstanding *noun*. A mistaken idea that a person gets because he or she did not understand what another person said or meant.

moderate *adjective*. Not overdone; using a small amount.

modestly *adverb*. In a manner that does not call attention to one's sex.

mysterious *adjective*. Like a mystery; hard to understand.

napkin *noun*. A large square of paper or cloth used to protect your clothing when you are eating, and to wipe your hands and mouth.

nickname *noun*. A short form of a name, or a familiar name that a person is called. *Mike is a nickname for Michael. Bill is a nickname for William.* An unofficial name that has been given to a person.

nude *adjective*. Without clothes.

nun [nuhn] *noun*. A "sister" in a religious order who does not marry, and lives a life serving her church and God.

obey *verb*. Follow a law or an order from someone.

occasion *noun*. Event; time.

odor *noun*. A smell.

offend *verb*. To hurt another's feelings, or make a person angry by one's words or actions.

offensive *adjective*. Rude; impolite; insulting; unpleasant.

offer *verb*. To ask someone if they would like something.

on behalf of *adverb*. As the representative of a group of people.

openness *noun*. An ability to speak directly and honestly, without hiding something.

opinion [oh pin′ yin] *verb*. A judgment; a person's feelings or thoughts about something.

overdo [oh′ver doo′] *verb*. To do more than needed.

party *noun*. A group that is traveling, eating, or doing some other activity together.

pasta *noun*. a form of spaghetti or macaroni, ziti, etc.

patient *noun*. A person who goes to a doctor because of an illness or injury.

pay attention *verb phrase*. To keep one's mind on a person or a conversation.

pedestrian [puh des′ tree uhn] *noun*. A person who is walking.

phony [foh′ nee] *adjective*. Not real; pretending to like someone that you don't really like.

pleasure *noun*. A good, happy feeling; joy and comfort.

polite *adjective*. Having good manners; kind, courteous.

possess [poh zes′] *verb*. To take over as one's own property.

posture [pahs′ chur] *noun*. The way a person stands or sits.

prayer *noun*. A conversation with God.

predictable *adjective*. Can be easy to guess what the person.

present [pree zent′] *verb*. Give.

prevent *verb*. To stop something from happening.

pride *noun*. A feeling of self-worth.

privately *adverb*. Alone; when no one else can see or hear you.

privilege [prih′ vuh lij] *noun*. A favor or advantage or right, that is not given to others. A person may have a privilege because of his or her age, money, sex, job, accomplishment, or position in society.

promotion *noun*. An advancement to a job with more responsibility and better pay.

pushy *adjective*. Aggressive; asking for things and taking things in a rude way, without thinking about others' needs; telling others what to do, without using polite manners.

put on a pedestal *idiom*. To treat like a beautiful statue.

rage *noun*. Extreme anger; uncontrolled fury.

recently *adverb*. Not too long ago; in the past few days (or years).

recklessly *adverb*. Without proper care; dangerously.

regional *adjective*. Based on the part of the country people are from.

register *verb*. To put one's name on a list; to go to a store and make a list of gifts that you would like.

respect 1. *noun*. The showing of good manners or kindness toward someone. 2 *verb*. To treat carefully; to be courteous to.

response *noun*. Answer.

retirement *noun*. The time when a person stops working, after working for many years.

right-of-way *noun*. The legal right to pass first, while other cars must slow or stop.

romance *noun*. An exciting love relationship.

rude [rood] *adjective*. Having bad manners; not polite.

run *verb*. To drip liquid or mucous. "I have a runny nose. My nose is running."

rush hour *noun phrase*. When the most people are on the road going to or coming home from work.

saint *noun*. A person with a special relationshp with God, according to the Roman Catholic church.

sarcastically *adverb*. [Speaking] in a way that you say the opposite of what you mean. This is in order to make an unkind joke or to show that you are annoyed. "Beautiful job, Claire!" (Claire has just spilled paint onto a new carpet.)

scam *noun*. A plan to get money by tricking a person with lies.

scold *verb*. To talk angrily to a child about his or her bad behavior.

second-hand smoke *noun phrase*. Smoke from another person, not oneself. Four thousand Americans die each year from *second-hand smoke*.

second helping *noun*. Another portion of food.

security *noun*. Protection against harm or thieves.

security guard *noun*. A person who keeps a school, hospital, airport, office building, etc., safe.

seldom *adverb*. Almost never.

self-confident *adjective*. Sure of one's worth.

semiprivate *adjective*. Shared by two patients.

senior *adjective*. The older one; the father whose son has the same name.

server, waiter, waitress *noun*. A person who serves food. The word *waitress* means a woman. The word *waiter* used to mean male, but now can refer to either male or female.

sexual harassment [huh ras′ ment] *noun phrase*. Repeated and unwanted actions or words of a sexual nature that bother, embarrass, insult, or upset another person.

silly *adjective*. Foolish; behaving stupidly.

sincere *adjective*. Honest; telling one's true feelings.

situation *noun*. A condition that a person is in: the place, the activity, and the other people. For example, in a classroom; at a supermarket; at a dinner with friends; at a job interview.

slurp *verb*. To make a noise while drinking or eating soup.

snack *noun*. A small amount of food.

sniff *verb*. To take a short, small breath in order to keep your nose from dripping or running when you have a cold.

sniffle *verb*. To make sniffing sounds when a nose is running; to cry quietly.

so-so *adverb*. Not good, not bad.

soul *noun*. The spirit part of a person that lives on after death.

spices *noun*. Pepper, herbs, onions, etc. that are added to food to give it extra flavor.

stare *verb*. To look at someone without moving your eyes away.

statistics *noun, plural*. A list of numbers: the games won and lost by each team, the batting averages, runs batted in, home runs, etc. of each player.

stroller *noun*. A small carriage in which a child sits.

strong opinions *noun, plural*. Ideas that you hold very strongly and that might be very different from the opinions of others.

supervisor *noun*. A person who is makes rules for, and is responsible for, a group of workers.

surname [sihr/ naym] Family name.

swallow *verb*. To move food from the mouth down into the stomach.

sweet *adjective*. Thoughtful; nice; kind.

sweethearts *noun, plural*. Two people in love with each other.

switch *verb*. To change or move.

sympathy *noun*. A showing of compassion for another person's problems or pain.

symptom *noun*. A sign of a sickness: fever, sneezing, rash, etc.

table manners *noun, plural*. The way people speak and act while eating.

tact *noun*. The ability to tell the truth without hurting a person's feelings.

telemarketer [tehl uh mar/kih tuhr] *noun*. A salesperson who uses the telephone to find customers.

tension *noun*. A feeling of stress because of differences of opinion, or anger about a matter.

tip *1. verb*. To give the server 15% or 20% of the check to pay for his or her service. *2. noun*. Money that is given to a worker for service.

title *noun*. A word such as *Mr., Mrs., Ms., Miss, Dr., Professor,* etc. used before a person's name.

tolerate *verb*. To accept without complaining.

tone of voice *noun phrase*. The quality of a person's voice. A tone can be soft, gentle, friendly, or pleasant. It can also be angry, sarcastic, harsh, threatening, or commanding.

topic *noun*. The subject of a conversation

total stranger *noun phrase*. A complete stranger. A person you have never met and never seen before.

touchy [tuh/ chee] *adjective*. Easily upset by what someone says or does.

traditionally *adverb*. In the way it was done in the past.

traffic jam *noun*. A condition on a road when cars either cannot move, or move very slowly.

transfer *verb*. To move from one job or class to another.

treat *verb*. To pay for someone else's dinner or other entertainment.

trim *verb*. To cut with a small pair of scissors.

twice *adverb*. Two times.

typical *adjective*. Usual, average.

undo [uhn doo] *verb*. Change something to the way it was before you did something to it.

unpleasant *adjective*. Not good; causing a bad feeling.

value *noun*. Something that a person considers to have importance or worth.

vehicle [vee′ uh kuhl] *noun*. A car, bus, motorcycle, truck, etc.

violence *noun*. Using force to hurt another person.

visiting hours *noun, plural*. The time when hospitals allow people to visit patients.

visitor's pass *noun*. A paper that gives a person permission to be in a hospital to visit a patient.

vulgar *adjective*. Having to do with sex, spoken in "dirty" language.

walk all over someone *idiom*. To take what one needs and wants without thinking about the needs or wishes of the other person.

weakness *noun*. A condition of having no strength or power.

well-mannered *adjective*. Having good behavior; able to speak and sit quietly.

whisper *verb*. To speak to someone very softly so others cannot hear.

wipe *verb*. To make a motion to clean something.

yawn *verb*. To open the mouth widely to get more air into the lungs when one is sleepy.

yield [yeeld] *verb*. To slow or stop in order to give another person or car the right to go first.

89

Notes